MY
CBD
MONEY TREE

Val -
The BEST is yet
to come !!

Renita Brannan

God Bless your
health !

DEDICATION

This book is dedicated to God, the incredible creator of this miraculous plant.

A special thanks to Dr Stuart Titus for being the first person to bring non-psychoactive CBD to the United States from Europe, after it had been demonized for 80 years. Your vision, hard work and bravery are changing millions of lives globally.

Thank you to Randy and Samantha Schroeder, our amazing friends and business partners, who helped us to launch our CBD business. If it weren't for your leadership and support, nothing in this book would have transpired. It was a divine appointment.

Thank you to my amazing husband Scott for helping me with this book and all of my projects that I believe will save and change lives! In addition, thanks to my boys, Beau, Truitt, and Rocco for always being an awesome example of God's goodness and excellence. You are all masterpieces.

Thank you to my mom and dad, Pearl and Richard Rhone for raising me with a strong work ethic and a servant's heart. Mom, your entrepreneur spirit helped all of us kids to be amazing business owners. Thanks to both of you for teaching us to garden and realize the power of plants to heal. Dad, thank you for teaching me to love and care for older people. Mom, thank you for teaching me to love animals, especially dogs. CBD has been a blessing for so many furry friends. Dad, thank you for giving me a love for the American soldier and flag and all of our freedoms we have in this great nation. Semper fi!

In conclusion, thank you to all of the amazing individuals featured in this book and those who continue to move the cannabis message to help heal the planet. Thank you for trusting Scott and me to help launch your business and help so many who desperately need it. The very best is yet to come!

CONTENTS

•

FOREWORDS

Foreword #1

Readers of "My CBD MONEY TREE" will learn from Renita Brannan, one of the most gifted entrepreneurs and personal health and fitness coaches in America. Learn how to put the end of the prohibition of cannabis to work in your life, whether as a consumer of products whose time has come or one who joins in the education and distribution process as an entrepreneur/business owner utilizing these remarkable health compounds.

This historic time is one of the most fascinating and important cultural changes in America and the world in the past seven decades. It is with fascination that I see becoming common place the use of plant compounds derived from cannabis that have been villainized, reviled and rendered illegal by an error in judgment made by governments around the world in the late 1930's.

Were a regulatory body today to state that oranges, grapefruit, lemons and limes were all the same, this would be an obvious error. While all citrus fruits, they are distinct in makeup, flavor, nutrients and use. The same is so for the two distinct sides of the cannabis family tree. The marijuana plant is grown principally for its psychoactive cannabinoid...THC. The industrial hemp plant is grown for a variety of purposes around the world, and today unique strains of hemp have been developed which contain high quantities of a therapeutic non-psychoactive cannabinoid, CBD. The error made in 1937 with the passing of the Marijuana Tax Act, which essentially designated two distinct plants with very different purposes as being one and the same was a mistake. A lime is not a lemon… and hemp is not marijuana!

I have invested my life identifying health and wellness related products whose time has come, and bringing those products to market. These products benefit both consumers and entrepreneurs who make possible the widespread distribution once identified and developed. Countless thousands of consumers have benefited from these product introductions and resulting sales volumes. This has eclipsed $3.5 billion over my career and has created wealth for many.

I invite you to devour, rather than peruse the pages of "My CBD MONEY TREE." When major cultural changes occur, wealth is created by those who see in advance the outcome and accelerate a process which is destined to occur.

Ask yourself this question… "Is the cannabis genie going to be put back in the bottle?" I think not. The continued unwinding of the prohibition of cannabis is a certainty. The error has been discovered. The process of unwinding that error is in full swing. In the following pages, you will learn how to put this set of facts to work to benefit you and your family for generations to come!

Randy Schroeder
Kannaway Crown Ambassador

Foreword #2

I remember arriving at the offices of Medical Marijuana, Inc. in March of 2016. I thought diligently about joining the company, especially having lived in areas of the country where cannabis was not well thought of. I sought the advice of many professionals and successful people in my circle of influence prior to joining the company. To my surprise, the advice was a resounding, "Do not let this opportunity pass you by."

As I considered joining Medical Marijuana, Inc and my role in leading Kannaway as its CEO, I remember distinctly one thought that I could not let go of. I looked around my home. I saw computers, clothing, phones, pictures, furniture, and the like. I asked myself if any of those industries would likely be larger 6 months from now or 6 years from now than they are today. Of course, I do not have a crystal ball and I do not know the answer to that question. However, I am certain of one thing; the cannabis industry will be larger 6 months from now. It will be larger 6 years from now and likely 60 years from now. Everyone wants to talk about cannabis. It is an exciting subject. It is being researched around the world for its benefits. It is being talked about and written about in media around the world. It is being legislated in various state and federal governments around the world. People want to talk about cannabis, and that makes being in this business so rewarding.

The next question was how to make Kannaway special. When I joined Kannaway as its CEO in March, 2016, it was one of only a handful of companies marketing a CBD based nutritional supplement. It's parent company,

Medical Marijuana, Inc. was the first company to ever launch a CBD product in the United States. To me, being new to the cannabis business the industry seemed to appear like the "Wild West." After participating in a few cannabis related events, it was clear to me. Kannaway had to become the professional company in an industry that is not always professional.

Kannaway's journey has been remarkable! From March 2016 through December 2019, the company grew its monthly revenue over 90 times. That is small in comparison to what we will we do in our future as we take the company and introduce CBD and other cannabis-based supplements around the world. I invite you to join Renita Brannan and her fast-growing team as we embark on a journey to change the world.

Blake Schroeder
Kannaway CEO

Foreword #3

Deregulation of Telecom & Energy… No contest!!

I've had the privilege of witnessing and participating in two of the biggest transfers of wealth this country has ever seen being part of telecom deregulation in the late 80's and early 90's and amazed at the fortune 500 companies that emerged from the baby Bell's. If that wasn't enough, years later I was able to witness and participate again in the deregulation of the electric and gas industries. Again, I was astounded by the emergence of billion-dollar companies almost overnight.

Never in my wildest dreams did I think anything else would fall on my plate and certainly within my lifetime to rival those two billion/trillion-dollar industries. In 2015 that's exactly what happened when a friend of mine sent me Kannaway products for my family to try. My wife had Lyme Disease for 26 years and chronic back pain for 4 years. He told me these products would help with her conditions. Of course, I was skeptical. Nothing had much effect on her back pain or disease including antibiotics.

Well two weeks later my wife was a different person and feeling 20 years younger. I was feeling more alive, waking up refreshed and wide awake! After those results, I started my CBD research and life changing journey!!
What a journey it has been!! I've been in the MLM industry for 30 years. As a founder, I helped start some of the biggest companies in the industry. I thought I had done and seen it all, until Kannaway!

Never in my 30 years have I seen anything like the deregulation, prohibition of the Cannabis/Hemp/Marijuana industry!! It makes the energy and telecom industries look like they are standing still. This worldwide movement is changing the lives of everyday people on a daily basis.

I'll be blatantly honest with you. When I joined Kannaway, I joined for two reasons. First, because of the life changing results I witnessed firsthand with my wife. Second, because of the STOCK PROGRAM the company offers Executives and top brand ambassadors who have earned specific ranks in the compensation plan. I had built billion-dollar companies for others. This was all about the results of the products and the stock, stock, stock.

After experiencing this powerful movement firsthand, now I realize, it's not about the stock. It has nothing to do with the stock. It's about changing people's lives by improving their health. I can honestly say I have helped more people in my last 3 years with Kannaway, than I did in my previous 27 years in the industry (and I have helped a lot of people in my previous 27 years).

What gets me up in the morning and commuting to San Diego from Michigan every week are the texts, emails and calls from people telling me our products have changed their lives. One of the biggest reasons we are changing so many people's lives is mega-entrepreneur, health coach and Kannaway Brand Ambassador Renita Brannan!! This powerhouse wife and mom of 3 boys has changed the way CBD is perceived in North Dakota and across the entire United States because of her efforts and the efforts of her fast-growing team! Renita has achieved one of the top ranks in our compensation plan in record time and today earning a monthly income people dream about. We are truly blessed to have her as a part of our company and look forward to the future together as we bring this misunderstood plant back to mainstream acceptance!

Brad Tayles
Kannaway VP of Operations

Foreword #4

When I first started around May of 2017 at that point things were very different. People were just starting to talk about CBD in the US and certainly not prevalent globally as the conversations were just starting to bubble and the buzz was building.

When I first met with the original founders, they cast a vision like I had never seen before. In my initial interviews we talked all about the power of Hemp and how it will be future commodity for people and needed for the planet. We talked about buying bankrupt cities and rebuilding in Hemp for low income families, Hemp batteries for buses, build first Hemp skyscrapers, Cannabis centric medical trainings and beyond. As we learn and research further into the complexity and utilization of this plant virtually most daily items can be replaced with Hemp and maintain a sustainable eco-friendly supply chain…win-win-win-win and Kannaway is the engine at the forefront.

That said we focused on European Union as the first international expansion target. At this point the CBD and Cannabis Laws in Europe were still fairly vague and unchallenged until we began our project. Our first critical step was to establish the risks and legal avenues to establish an instant full European expansion into the 28 member states in one release. After meeting with top MLM legal counsel we quickly realized we were entering uncharted waters and would be the company to trailblaze the industry in Europe.

This started an unprecedented chapter for the industry

with Kannaway becoming the first Cannabis based MLM to enter Europe and also this put us as the first truly international Cannabis business. As a part of our mission it was important to create an organic and local operation. We immediately began to build a localized European infrastructure and supply chain. It was important of us to be invested in local Hemp industry both for sales and to help develop new opportunities for local Hemp entrepreneurs.

Very quickly the sales boomed to outpace our production and forced us to scale very quickly. Since the launch end of 2017 we have now developed a CBD business putting us in the top 5 CBD companies in Europe and unequivocally the top CBD MLM in Europe experiencing +50% growth year over year (2018 vs.2019). Throughout the process of navigating the ever-changing regulations we faced many challenges and significant obstacles. One of which was the announcement of the Austrian authorities that they believed all CBD is deemed illegal and subject to prosecution for those involved in the selling or promoting CBD based products. This announcement came months before our scheduled major function in Austria. We had a decision to make to cancel/postpone the convention or to stay the course as we planned. The ultimate decision was made to continue the mission and create an event focused solely on Hemp education and activism. This gave birth to the Hemp for Humanity project.

Hemp for Humanity became the war cry for our message for countries that still have CBD restrictions. This project focuses on the power of Hemp for wellness, the planet, humanitarian and business. We have now taken this message to Russia, now becoming the first ever legally registered CBD product, went to Turkey meeting the highest government officials to discuss the future of CBD for the Middle East region resulting in Helal and Kosher certifications.

Hemp for Humanity has now spread to Asia with Japan as the initial entry point where executed some of the first ever Hemp based education seminars in Japan educating parliament officials and distinguished members of the medical community. Finally, recently, held a Hemp for Humanity conference in Iceland with hundreds of professionals and government officials to further educate the local population to ultimately lift the CBD restrictions and help support lobbying CBD access to their communities.

The global opportunities are growing at a rapid rate and we will continue to stress the regulatory system to force conversation about the need to have safe and standardized guidelines to protect this important industry and consumers. That said we have pushed to obtain one of the first ever administered Free Sale Certificates for a CBD supplement in Bulgaria which made international news and set new precedent for the industry and we are working on more registrations to follow.

As I look to the future there is no other commodity space on the planet like Cannabis and Hemp centric product development. The world is ready for a change to sustainable products that focus on natural holistic wellness and sustainability for our planet.

With Kannaway at the forefront of the global movement

our competitive edge is a decade of research and development which lends our credibility to get our foot in the door at the highest levels of decision making in order to continue to create a change and opportunity. Kannaway and the message of Hemp For Humanity is now spreading all over the world and the need for our products and opportunity is vital.

Alex Grapov
Kannaway Chief Sales Operator

INTRODUCTION

The Green Rush and Financial Opportunities

A worldwide revolution is upon us – the movement that many call "The Green Rush", the near-term end of cannabis prohibition. Positive experience by the masses is changing the way people of the world today think about cannabis. The propaganda of the past is being replaced by the realization that cannabis is beneficial, and that the science of cannabis supports its use. Soon the end of Cannabis Prohibition will be upon us and the trends are showing many similarities that parallel the end of (failed) Alcohol Prohibition from December 1933.

History has been said to "repeat itself" and this was nowhere more apparent to me in the early stages of my career. I had been a bond trader and underwriter on Wall Street since 1979 but had also been following the stock market and some of the individuals who were somewhat expert in charting market movements, stock trading patterns, etc. As we approached the summer of 1987, a fellow who had been an "Elliott Wave" chartist, Robert Prechter was sounding a great alarm. Prechter's analysis was in overlaying the trading patterns of the stock market crash in 1929 along with the current trading patterns in 1987 – the overlays were eerily similar. If true, the predictions for the balance of 1987 would be for an historic crash in stock prices as measured by the Dow Jones average. Sure enough, the stock market crashed in October 1987 as predicted by the 1929 charts – in an incredibly similar manner.

In 1929, the stock market crash was a leading indicator of

future economic activity and it was ten rough years before the US began to recover from the Great Depression, led by increased military activity and expenditures for World War I. In 1987, America's corporations who had seen their share prices decline by over 50% from summer 1987 through year end – started buying back their shares on the open market with excess cash reserves. This brought stability to financial markets and created an atmosphere of optimism – that company's thought their best investment was back in themselves and their future prospects. Over the 32 years since the stock market crash in 1987, the Dow Jones averages have risen more than 1000% or over ten times in value (year-end 1987 – December 2018).

In terms of the current reform and acceptance of cannabis – we are seeing similar parallels to the end of Alcohol Prohibition in the United States. Here is a summary:

To draw some parallels with the end of Alcohol Prohibition, let's start with the 18th Amendment to the US Constitution which created Alcohol Prohibition – this passed the US States with 75%+ majority on January 29, 1919. The law took effect one year later. The 18th Amendment had been submitted in 1917, during World War I, as the US wanted to save its grain production for war efforts – in a move led by President Woodrow Wilson. In October 1919, with the necessary US State votes at hand, Congress passed the National Prohibition Act which provided guidelines for the federal enforcement of Alcohol Prohibition.

Franklin Delano Roosevelt was elected President of the

United States in November 1932 and his victory meant the beginning of the end of Alcohol Prohibition. Roosevelt's Presidential Platform included "Ending Alcohol Prohibition" – post election he lobbied Congress and the US States – he was soon thereafter successful at Constitutional Reform. With the country deep into the Depression Era – a new platform to create jobs and generate revenue by legalizing the alcohol industry carried an undeniable appeal to the downtrodden US population. FDR easily defeated incumbent President Herbert Hoover in November 1932 and took office in January 1933.

Ending Alcohol Prohibition was brought up for Congressional vote and in February 1933 Congress adopted a resolution proposing a 21st Constitutional Amendment that would then repeal the 18th Amendment. This Amendment was submitted to the US States and in December 1933, Utah provided the 36th and final necessary vote for ratification of the 21st Amendment to the US Constitution, thus ending Alcohol Prohibition. At the time there were 48 US States, thus Utah's vote provided the 75% majority necessary for Constitutional Amendment #21 to pass (36 of 48 US States, or 75% had approved).

The Prohibition of Alcohol proved difficult to enforce and further proved BAD for the economy, as restaurants lost sales and revenues, creating further job losses during already difficult economic times (The Great Depression). Manufacturers and distributors of alcohol turned to the illegal, illicit market and became known as "bootleggers". Crime rose during Prohibition – it made criminals out of formerly law-abiding citizens and those crime bosses such as Al Capone, thrived by providing illicit activities, reportedly making over $60 million annually. "Speakeasies" provided the masses with underground access to alcohol, the interstate transport of home-produced alcohol (known as "moonshine") created an "underground economy".

FDR supposedly celebrated the end of Alcohol Prohibition by drinking a "dirty martini", which was his favorite adult beverage. Does any of this sound familiar to today's cannabis prohibition and developing US cannabis markets? Affirmative I say.

As of December 2019, in the United States we now have 33 US States with Medical Cannabis laws on their books and 11 US States that allow for recreational use of cannabis (adult use of cannabis). We are nearing this 75%+ majority in a similar manner as happened during the end of Alcohol Prohibition– should there be a Constitutional Amendment favoring legalizing cannabis, it would require 38 of the 50 US States to vote favorably.

The great experiment of recreational cannabis in Colorado began with a majority of Colorado's voters approving Amendment 64 on November 6, 2012. Recreational cannabis sales began on January 1, 2014 and this has proven to be incredibly successful for the State of Colorado. Governor John Hickenlooper, formerly against cannabis but a champion of the will of the majority has even become a convert, using his power to keep DEA and federal law enforcement out of Colorado – except for when too much "supposedly legally grown cannabis" exited the backdoor of these grow-ops and found its way to the cannabis black market.

It should also be noted that Washington state also passed a voter referendum in November 2012 to legalize cannabis. The Washington program rollout started in July 2014. Similar to alcohol, cannabis prohibition created a significant "underground economy" with black market cannabis sales possibly exceeding $120 billion annually in the US. The major beneficiaries have been the drug cartels from south of the US border, but it should also be noted that the majority of prisoners in US jails are there for marijuana related offenses.

The experiments of recreational cannabis in Colorado and Washington have proved to be successful beyond even the most optimistic of the scenarios. Crime is down by nearly 20% in these cannabis-friendly US States. Tax revenues are soaring. Colorado in 2018 may generate as much as $300 million in tax receipts from medical and recreational cannabis sales. Employment is rising, jobs are being created and there is NO SIGN of any economic slowdown or recession in Colorado.

So, for those who are looking for opportunity in a newly emerging industry – the reform of cannabis and its growing acceptance provides such incredible potential, seen once every 100 years. Imagine if you owned stock or other ownership in alcohol companies such as Jim Beam, Seagram's, Anheuser-Busch before the end of alcohol prohibition? Now imagine owning shares in some of today's emerging cannabis companies!!

In the financial markets today, we are seeing incredible amounts of money being raised by Canadian Licensed Producers (LP's). Here, cannabis and its recreational use became legal on October 17, 2018 and their regulatory authority, Health Canada had previously allowed for a select group of "Licensed Producers" – those with the federal approval to cultivate, supply and distribute cannabis legally and lawfully. In 2018, these Canadian LPs have raised over $10 billion of investor capital.

Everyone seems to be focused on the THC market, as the underground "Black Market" for recreational cannabis has been developing since the early 1960's. Today we estimate this "Black Market" for cannabis to be $120 billion in the US and worldwide about $240 billion annually.

In 2012, a group of entrepreneurs based in San Diego California introduced a new form of cannabis – a nutraceutical hemp-based cannabidiol (CBD) product that quickly spread throughout the US and world markets. CBD had been formerly known as "The Hippie's Disappointment" as progressive marijuana growers tried growing a high concentration CBD form of marijuana – however when smoked, there was no psychoactive effect (unlike THC) and thus CBD was recognized by hippies as "the thing that gave you a headache".

According to US Government research, CBD is a non-psychoactive cannabinoid (see US Patent # 6630507) and is also preferable to utilize therapeutically, as it avoids the intoxicating effects of the psychoactive cannabinoids. Thus, one can take much higher amounts of CBD (several milligrams) without any psychedelic or intoxicating effects. Many can take 100 mgs CBD and be mentally alert, drive an automobile and not fail a drug screening. As little as 3 – 5 mgs of THC can have people sleeping for many hours (a phenomena known as "couch lock syndrome").

The emergence of this nutraceutical form of cannabis, CBD, was initially met with skepticism, particularly from those within the cannabis industry. Many seasoned Pro's mentioned that "you can't get CBD from hemp". It was fun to watch these long-time hemp guys change their tune once CBD sales started to outpace hemp food product sales. Instead of smoking a CBD form of marijuana, consumers could now potentially benefit from hemp and the CBD-rich extracts that were developed into more socially acceptable ingestible and topical application forms. Here consumers would potentially be able to get 25, 50 and maybe even 100 mgs of CBD daily to benefit health and wellness – all without the stigma of smoking a cannabis cigarette (aka "joint").

Over the next 6 years, CBD has become "The Next BIG Thing" according to many news sources. Sales of CBD are projected to reach $1.2 billion by 2019 (Forbes) thus making it worth about 1% of the overall cannabis marketplace. But CBD's appeal is quite mainstream – people can potentially get health and wellness benefits without the "high" associated with THC. The New York Times, CNN and Time Magazine now announce that "CBD is everywhere".

The discovery and emergence of the human body's endogenous cannabinoid system (1988) has been one of the most profound discoveries in the history of science and medicine. Far underappreciated for its self-regulatory significance – this system governs about every physiological action in the human body. Our human bodies produce our own internal, endogenous cannabinoids as well. These internal cannabinoids are quickly degraded by enzymatic activities – however plant-based cannabinoids can hold a much longer "shelf life" in the human body. This has potential benefits for many who are suffering with "Clinical Endocannabinoid Deficiency" a concept and term characterized by Dr. Ethan Russo in 2003.

Supplementing the human body's endogenous cannabinoid system has proven to be a huge benefit for many seeking higher levels of health and wellness. When one looks at the huge receptor network within our bodies for cannabinoids – it stands to reason that these plant cannabinoids may be beneficial for you. Our belief is that these non-psychoactive cannabinoids are absolutely vital and necessary nutrients that support the optimal function of the human body. Soon we hope to establish a recommended daily intake.

Many of our colleagues have come to benefit from introducing CBD to others and from this, we have created an opportunity for the distribution of CBD via a network marketing company, known as Kannaway. Formed in April 2014, Kannaway had a huge initial reception, but was unable to deliver all the product that there was initial demand for, had problems with merchant processing and paying representatives (known as Brand Ambassadors) on a timely basis. Due to overall cannabis prohibition, access to banking and merchant processing services has been an incredible challenge within the industry. Kannaway almost died out in early 2016, but in March of that year – corporate executives decided to bring in more experienced management.

Today Kannaway thrives! Having established a fully THC-free form of CBD, Kannaway was resurrected throughout the United States and started informal operations in Europe in December 2017. Currently boasting about 94,000 Brand Ambassadors worldwide, Kannaway has presented financial opportunity for those selling and recruiting others to do so.

Kannaway also provides funding for a non-profit group known as ECHO Connection, where many in financial need can obtain charitable access to CBD products. Many of the ECHO families are grateful for the improvements in health and wellness by taking CBD nutraceutical products. To begin in Kannaway, one does not need millions of dollars, as would be required to start a cannabis-based enterprise. Many have developed an excellent income to where they are replacing their former salaries – and are now doing Kannaway on a full-time basis. Not enough research exists yet on the benefits of the nutraceutical form of CBD in order for anyone in the industry to "make product claims", to show that nutraceutical CBD products treat, mitigate or diagnose illness or medical conditions. However, recently the US FDA did approve an isolated form of CBD mixed with an oil – Epidiolex, which is used for children with drug-resistant forms of epilepsy. Shares of stock in this early stage pharmaceutical company could have been purchased in May 2014 for $10 a share when they entered the US marketplace. Recently such shares have traded hands as high as $160 per share. Early investors have profited handsomely.

The large Canadian Licensed Producers are raising billions of dollars, some of the pharmaceutical companies in the cannabinoid space have raised hundreds of millions of dollars. Start-up operations in many US States with a state-based license will run into the millions of dollars to open the doors of a new business, with the hope of returning many more millions to investors. Through Kannaway, opportunities are now available for the entrepreneur – and certainly those who were early believers in the remake of Kannaway from March 2016 have done remarkably well financially.

We like to believe that the "trend is our friend" and that many of us within the cannabis industry will make our fortunes. Many of the biggest fortunes may still be made by companies that have not even started yet – thus everything (in our estimation) within the overall cannabis industry remains very ground floor level.

Herein, one will find the story of an enterprising woman, a rather typical but highly motivated American woman who has built a career and reputation as a personal trainer plus nutrition coach. When she found out about CBD and its potential health-providing benefits – her life took a major shift. She has helped many to achieve health and wellness, plus provided opportunity to her growing network of Brand Ambassadors.

Like many of us – when Renita Brannan found out the truth about cannabis and realized that the research side of the US Government held a patent on the therapeutic use of its extracts (cannabinoids) and that hemp was the basis for the early American economy – there was no turning back. She today marches forward after enduring risking prosecution in her state daily – like many do in the industry. I vividly remember the first time we shipped a nutraceutical hemp-based CBD cannabis product across US State lines. With legal opinion letters firmly in hand – there were many sleepless nights. When the DEA declared CBD to be a Schedule 1 federally controlled substance – we had further "bulls-eye's" on our backs in the industry. Our response: DEA you did not even follow your own rules to so establish CBD as a Schedule 1. Again, we all flew in the face of danger. Innumerable bank accounts, merchant processing accounts have been shut down. The challenge of renting an apartment, buying a home or doing most anything economically (receiving a paycheck) has been extraordinary difficult.

On the positive side, Consumer Reports recently surveyed more than 4000 individuals. More than 25% of people in the United States say they have tried CBD. Most of those who have tried CBD reported that it was effective, especially among those who used for anxiety. In some cases (22% of the people) said, CBD allowed them to eliminate over-the-counter or prescription drugs, including opioids. 75% of the people who took CBD said it was at least moderately effective for the main reason they took it, with 48% saying it was extremely effective. (Consumer Reports- April 2019) Most of these people surveyed did not find out about CBD from their doctor, rather they found out about CBD and where to obtain products through their friends, family or via the internet.

Forbes reports that the average American starting a course of CBD therapy takes 2.8 pharmaceutical pills per day. Four months after starting a course of CBD nutraceutical products, the average person now takes 0.7 pharmaceutical pills per day.

Cannabis is potentially disruptive to the alcohol, tobacco, pharmaceutical, and possibly to the food and beverage industries. In Colorado, alcohol sales are down by 15% since recreational cannabis was legalized and tobacco sales are close behind. Many leading companies in these arenas are investing billions alongside cannabis companies to find a way to recapture lost market share – and to stay ahead of future trends which may leave them well behind the curve, if they do not keep up with the cannabis reform movement.

On December 20, 2018, U.S. President Donald Trump signed the Agricultural Improvement Act of 2018 (aka the 2018 Farm Bill). This legislation holds tremendous implications for industrial hemp and its derivatives.

First, hemp will no longer be part of the Controlled Substances Act and brought back to the American Farmer as an approved agricultural crop for the first time in 82 years (since the marijuana Tax Act of 1937). Hemp will be allowed to be planted by farmers under the direction of the US Department of Agriculture with the full program launching in the spring of 2020.

Farmers will be able to obtain crop insurance for hemp – and we expect that a hemp futures market will develop enabling hemp futures to be traded on the Chicago Board of Trade, right next to wheat, corn, oats, soybeans, etc.

The Agricultural Improvement Act of 2018 also legalizes the derivatives of hemp, including CBD. This will have a significant impact on the emerging CBD markets as many grey-areas in the lawfulness have been cleared up. The US FDA will have to make a pathway for now descheduled CBD to be listed as a food ingredient, dietary supplement – or both.

While I am writing this, 42 (growing every month) US States have hemp laws on their books, so we can envision as much as 60 million acres of US farm property being planted with hemp. Many would say that as the US goes, so goes the world – and we do expect significant international opportunities to emerge with the new US stance on hemp and CBD.

Forbes is projecting 2019 US CBD sales to approach $1.2 billion and CNBC now reports that CBD sales by 2022 may approach $22 billion. For us within the CBD industry, this is a very exciting time with the CBD industry making national and international news on a daily basis.

We look forward to the months and years ahead – and wish you great enjoyment with the story at hand. The end of cannabis prohibition only comes once in a lifetime and certainly there are interesting parallels to the end of alcohol prohibition. Many of us "old-timers" know that "history repeats itself" – certainly there are fantastic financial opportunities awaiting entrepreneurs within the cannabis industry and many have already made early fortunes within this arena.

We have seen fortunes made in industries such as financial mergers and acquisitions, real estate, dotcoms, technology and the rest. There have not been any real opportunities since the dot com era and its bubble of 2000. The cannabis sector will present the next great wave of fortune-making and early investors have already cashed in on to a degree.

Prediction: the best days of the entire cannabis industry lie ahead. We encourage enterprising entrepreneurs to get a piece of the action and stake your claim in the new era of cannabis reform. This type of mega-opportunity only happens about once in a century.

Wishing you good health,

Dr. Stuart W Titus
President & CEO
Medical Marijuana Inc. (OTC: MJNA)
America's First Publicly Traded Cannabis Company

CHAPTER 1

GREENRUSH IS THE NEW GOLDRUSH

Why did you pick up this book? Is it because you are intuitive and can feel the shifting of our country's healthcare system? Have you heard of the many "CBD miracles?" Are you searching for a lucrative opportunity within the cannabis space and don't know where to begin? This historic time is being called the GREENRUSH! People are talking about it WORLDWIDE!! The health and wealth of many sharp "risk takers" are about to skyrocket!

You are watching all of this, thinking IT'S MY TURN! You want to feel better! You want a part of this!! You hunger for success! You want time and financial freedom! You are FINALLY in the right place at the right time.

Let's talk CBD!

You are about to learn how to grow your CBD Money Tree!

3 Ways to Make Money with Cannabis:

1. Farming Hemp (*marijuana is very different than hemp and is illegal to grow in many states)
2. Own a Dispensary/Storefront
3. Launch a Global Kannaway CBD Business

1. Farming Hemp

Farming hemp is a legitimate way to capitalize on the impending explosive growth of this incredible CBD opportunity. Let's acknowledge the obvious first, not everyone is a farmer. I grew up on a little hobby farm. I was a strong, athletic teenager but was not active in any sports because of the responsibilities at home. Many spring and summer days were spent picking rocks, watering tree rows, manuring the barn, pail feeding calves, painting fences, planting and weeding the garden. I was taught in middle school Earth Science class that the earth is made up of layers of rocks. Huh? It finally makes sense why that job of "picking rocks" was never completely done! While many of my relatives are amazing farmers with great agricultural businesses, I'm not going to pretend to know or teach you what it will take to be a successful farmer growing hemp. To be honest, I have a heck of a time keeping plants alive. Maybe it's because I don't have a green thumb or maybe it's because farming is just not my passion.

However, let's talk about some of the many challenges farmers must overcome when raising a quality hemp product. First, hemp is a "bio-accumulator" and "phytoremediator" - meaning everything in the air and ground is absorbed by the plant itself. As a bio-accumulator, the farmer will be challenged to produce a "clean crop." As hemp collects and stores pesticides and chemical toxins from both the air and soil it becomes unsuitable to extract CBD oil. The variety of the hemp plant that's used for phytoremediation is also dangerous and not suitable for products like CBD. Keep in mind, the vast majority of all crops grown in the United States are genetically modified organisms (GMO). It takes several years to reestablish the soil before growing clean hemp. Naturally, clean hemp is the only source for quality, safe, effective CBD.

Of course, if there's a race to get CBD products to market (to cash in on the greenrush), I wonder if the farmer would examine the environment and soil carefully before planting? What was planted in that field last year? Hopefully not a GMO corn, soy, or wheat crop. How many years has the land been abused with chemicals? Is the hemp crop close to pollution or industry of any kind where the air/soil could be contaminated? I grew up 2 miles from a power plant and watched the smokestacks pour out thick black smoke daily. I remember thinking to myself, "that can't be good for the air quality". As hemp absorbs these toxins from the air, you would never want a crop cultivated for CBD in these environmental conditions.

Another challenge is the limited seed supply. Currently, there are only a few places to obtain high quality hemp seed. Until recently, seeds were only available in Canada and Europe. The challenge is the 0.3% THC limit. There is also some question about how imported seed will acclimate to latitudes and what the result will be at harvest. Imagine investing your start-up capital in seed that yields a hemp crop exceeding the 0.3% THC limit! It would be considered marijuana and under federal law must be destroyed. It will take some time to get a good feel for how those genetics express themselves in different environments.

Although dependent on goals of the farmer, one should invest in hemp seeds that have been produced from a consistent source for several years and have been grown by other farmers locally through previous seasons. This is very difficult as few farmers in the United States have been growing hemp successfully. It's kind of a shot in the dark for many beginner hemp farmers. Will the hemp they plant even be viable? With many people focusing on the lucrative potential with the passing of the 2018 Farm Bill, it is more important than ever before to secure high-quality hemp seeds. We have heard numerous stories already of many farmers who are seeking fast cash and quickly purchasing seeds from questionable sources. Although the greenrush has just begun, quality and safety are a few of the biggest challenges when looking at CBD from hemp. It all starts with the soil and the environment where the hemp will be grown.

Another major problem few are aware of with farming hemp is appropriate sun exposure. If hemp is not harvested timely and left in the sun just a few days too long, THC content increases. This recently happened in California and Hawaii. Millions of dollars of hemp crop were destroyed by the DEA as the THC content exceeded the federal limit. If the hemp crop tests at a mere .3% THC, it is currently illegal in our country. The hemp fields in California recently seized and destroyed by DEA tested at 1%. Many hemp farmers do not have reliable insurance yet due to confusion about legalization. Imagine spending all that time, energy, and money planting a hemp field, just to have the DEA burn it as the THC concentration is too high! Worse yet, imagine selling to consumers who were drug tested and you didn't realize the CBD extracted from your hemp contained elevated THC concentration! People will lose their jobs because of your negligence in understanding how the sun affects this crop. Sounds like too much stress for me.

We've discovered farming operations in Europe who have focused on hemp for centuries. They have the highest quality, safest, and most effective CBD hemp crops in the world. These farmers in Europe have higher "quality control" and true love for the integrity and protection of the land. There are far less genetically modified crops in Europe. According to www.gmoanswers.com, the United States is the LARGEST PRODUCER of genetically modified crops in the entire world. Approximately 92% of our corn, 94% of our soybeans, 93% of our cotton, 90% canola, and 100% of sugar beets are all GMO crops. How healthy is the US soil you might be wondering? I am asking the same question.

Next, you'll have to grow hemp in a state where it's legal. Prepare to research long and hard. The state codes are virtually written in Greek. Most documents are so long and have so many amendments, it almost takes an attorney to decode the verbiage. Although Trump signed the 2018 Farm Bill, many states still have not rewritten their state codes to allow planting of hemp. Do your research if you want to become a hemp farmer.

Since the goal of this book is to help you grow your very own CBD MONEY TREE, let's look at what farming hemp is going to cost you. According to www.wikileaf.com, the average cost of starting a legal growery is $20,000 start-up and average annual fees for a "medium indoor growery" is around $78,000. Licensing fees associated with the state you plan to grow the crop average $4,000. Currently, it's estimated only 1% of growers are licensed. Why? Because they can't afford the cost.

MY CBD MONEY TREE – Checklist

Hemp Farmer
1. Products that can potentially help a broad range of people?
+ Yes
2. Potential to earn massive income?
+ Yes
3. Anyone can do it or small learning curve?
- No. Definitely not.
Reality check. Extensive research and testing need to be done to plant a quality, clean, safe, bountiful hemp CBD harvest.
4. Low start-up cost and low monthly business obligation?
- No
Over $20k and expenses running upwards to over $100k... Not exactly what I had in mind!

5. Legal?
+/- Yes/No
Even where it's legal in the US, 99% of growers are operating illegal businesses. Major red flags here.

Honestly, we didn't even touch on lending from banks to start your "hemp farm", which is a steep mountain to climb due to current banking regulations. Too much labor and headache involved… Next!

Final thought: We also didn't discuss environmental conditions like hail, wind, drought, or excessive rain – all which affect our crops. Mother Nature can be cruel. This is massive risk!

2. Own a Cannabis Dispensary/Storefront

Owning a marijuana dispensary or storefront, like owning any traditional business, consists of operating that location, owning or leasing the space, carefully selecting inventory, making sure your cannabis is not moldy from your suppliers, getting quality product that have a Certificate of Analysis (COA), negotiating product quantity and price (including shipping), advertising budget, initial product orders and month to month inventory management, an interviewing process to select trustworthy and hardworking employees, training your new staff, and security and counter-theft measures.

With opening a cannabis storefront, the preceding list is something to be deeply researched and considered before thinking a dispensary is the way to go. Owning or leasing is not a small expense. If you want to keep it "mom and pop", you are still looking at elevated expense as "bricks and mortar" businesses many times consume most of the owner's time, energy, and money to get it up and growing. With so much of the world now moving to online purchasing, it makes the marketplace more competitive, which leaves the small business owner with little to no profits if they are considering a high-quality CBD. Honestly, opening a storefront would be a large risk, but opening a medical marijuana dispensary would be even greater.

The application fee for a marijuana dispensary will set you back $1,000 to $10,000 depending on the state you're operating in. In several states, your non-refundable application fee is subject to a lottery drawing. How would you like to drop $10,000 and find out you weren't selected? Don't worry, the state won't have any problems spending your money. In the rare event you are selected in the lottery, you'll then pay a licensing fee between $4,000 and $120,000 depending on the estimated value of your operation. You'll need to factor in real estate, which can cost from $50,000 - $1,000,000+ depending on geographic location.

Maybe the biggest challenge in owning a dispensary or storefront is "banking and insurance". Federal and state banking regulations have not fully opened to marijuana dispensary/storefront owners. Don't plan on borrowing money or purchasing liability insurance to help you launch your business or cover your risk. In most cases, it's all upfront cash on your end! When it comes to selling product, many times it's also a cash deal. This "cash only" environment creates risk and potential dangers including theft and violence. This sounds like too much stress for me.

MY CBD MONEY TREE – Checklist

Dispensary Owner
1. Products that can potentially help a broad range of people?
+ Yes
2. Potential to earn massive income?
+ Yes
3. Anyone can do it and small learning curve?
- No
Everyone wants to own a retail store, until you own a retail store… Especially in the cannabis space. Due to fear, ignorance and controversy, this is big hill to climb. All work and no play with bills piling up is a serious responsibility to consider before jumping in.
4. Low start-up cost and low monthly business obligation?
- No. Incredibly costly.
Real estate expenses, licensing fees, employees, payroll taxes, high inventory and shipping costs. This will take very deep pockets.
5. Legal?
+/- Yes or No
When selecting a company's products to sell in your retail store, be sure the vendor is following all the federal and state laws. Be sure they have third party testing on the products to ensure purity and quality including % of CBD and THC. Definitely make sure you are not getting "moldy" cannabis. Be certain to only purchase products that have a Certificate of Analysis (COA). Keep in mind, many COA's list the amount of CBD, THC, CBG, etc. but fail to "test" the heavy metals such as arsenic and lead. Instead on their COA, it will say N/A which means NOT AVAILABLE meaning THEY DID NOT TEST!

Now that is scary! If you are looking at a COA with a line of N/A's, that is not the quality product that you would want to consume or sell. Be very particular about quality, safety, efficacy, and COA's.

It's understandable as cannabis has been a negative stigma in the United States since around 1937. However, I hated being at the mercy of federal and state lawmakers, who are mostly overwhelmed and uneducated regarding cannabis. I don't want to deal with "employees" handling cash deals. That just sounds like a fire waiting to happen. The banking system is "currently" not set up for the cannabis or hemp entrepreneur to win.

Honestly, I just want to help as many people as I can and have a business that creates revenue and profit right out of the gate!

3. Launch a Global Kannaway CBD Business

Launching a global Kannaway CBD business is easy to get started. The annual membership fee is $55 plus your business value pack. The cost is dependent on your financial goals. The value packs range in price from $699 - $1,999. My husband, Scott, and I selected the $1,999 Total Product Experience package as we had big goals and understood the value of experiencing each and every product firsthand. Plus, we really wanted THE TOTAL PRODUCT EXPERIENCE!

The $55 annual membership fee includes an incredibly beautiful personalized website, the Kannaway Connect app, and the ability to track your team, commissions, order history, training, clinical studies on cannabis, detailed lab results on our products, and marketing materials.

Your monthly expense is just the cost of your personal smart-ship order (less than $200 per month). This is a small but important monthly investment to have the opportunity to operate a global business with potential of earning well over 6 figures per year!

Kannaway has a program called "3 for free" in which you can earn FREE additional monthly product if you have 3 customers a month. The best part is they can be the same 3 customers every month. You know what is better than the best quality, triple lab tested CBD? The best quality, triple lab tested CBD for FREE!

Here's an important question to answer when launching any type of business. How long will it take to cover my start-up expenses? Personally, I paid back our $2,000 startup expense in just 3 days! (Keep in mind, I wasn't even an expert in cannabis yet!)

Kannaway's parent company (MJNA) is the FIRST and ONLY company with hemp CBD listed in the Physicians Digital Reference (formerly known as the Physician's Desk Reference) which is a reference for Physicians and various health care providers regarding both pharmaceuticals and nutraceuticals. Kannaway's products stand alone in quality and purity.

MY CBD MONEY TREE – Checklist

Kannaway Brand Ambassador

1. Products that can potentially help a broad range of people?
+ Yes
2. Potential to earn massive income?
+ Yes
3. Anyone can do it and small learning curve?
+ Yes
4. Low start-up cost and low monthly business obligation?
+ Yes
5. Legal?
+ Yes

To be associated with the very first publicly traded cannabis stock (MJNA) in the United States is a special honor. To represent the highest quality cannabis products on the planet is incredibly powerful. To witness lives positively impacted physically from these products is life changing. To help families create massive financial wealth is a worthy mission! Motivated people are stepping up to the plate! This is a once in a lifetime opportunity. This is the greenrush baby!

CHAPTER 2

WE ARE GOING TO KAUAI BOYS!

My family and I recently enjoyed a truly amazing vacation. For a family living in landlocked North Dakota enduring months of frigid cold winds, ice and snow, nothing is more amazing and healing than warm sun, palm trees, sandy beaches, local pacific-rim food, island adventures, crashing waves, family time, and meeting new friends.

On this epic trip to Kauai, HI we were welcomed at the airport with smiles and a flower-filled lei for each family member. We were escorted to a 5-star resort where we "set up camp" for the week. Our room's balcony flaunted a perfect view of the ocean. The first morning we woke to a sunrise that will leave a beautiful imprint on our mind for years to come. Sounds of crashing waves, joy and laughter filled the room. After a wonderful island breakfast, we planned our week. What a surreal and wonderful blessing for our family!

We hiked through Jurassic terrain in the Waimea Canyon State Park, above the clouds and through vast canyons and multiple waterfalls. We skimmed across the Pacific Ocean on a 48-foot Catamaran along the NaPali coast, one of the tallest and most beautiful coastlines in the world. We leaned over and touched the clear turquoise blue water as hundreds of Hawaiian Spinner Dolphins cruised playfully in our wake. We dined at the prestigious oceanfront Beach House restaurant in Poipu gazing at a majestic sunset which seemed like just a skipped rock away. As the team of waiters and waitresses offered impeccably good old-fashioned Hawaiian hospitality, we looked up to see thousands (and I mean thousands) of beautiful green parrots dive into the trees above to nest for the night.

Our youngest boys, Tru and Rocco, went scuba diving for the very first time. We splashed and sunbathed all day, enjoyed team pool volleyball with music rockin', then more down time in the sun, relaxing, with cool drinks and great books. We boogie boarded, snorkeled and even won the Beach Olympics with new friends from Europe.

Can you imagine a vacation like this? What does your dream vacation look like?
Where is it that you want to go? Who do you want to take with you?

We earned the trip I just described in the first 28 days of our Kannaway business. We told our boys to buckle up when we signed up with Kannaway. We knew it was going to be a great adventure! We had our eyes on that trip from day one! On the 28th day of being part of Kannaway, we picked the boys up from school and said,

"Pack your snorkels, we just won a trip to Kauai!!" The boys screamed with excitement! It was an incredible blessing to our family!

Have you ever earned a trip in your first month of working at your job? How would you like to earn trips around the world to remarkable locations with amazing people who are having a blast making a huge physical/financial difference?

CHAPTER 3

DECIDE WHERE YOU ARE GOING

Sometimes moving forward means taking a step back. If you made the mistake of passing over the forward and epilogue of this book, I encourage you to start again. GO READ IT!!! The info packed within those first few short pages is LIFECHANGING! Sometimes in life it's changing the people you surround yourself with. The amazing visionaries who contributed to MY CBD MONEYTREE changed our lives! I want you to get to know these leaders. They can change your life too! Think of it as a divine appointment you don't want to miss.

Scott and I learned many years ago (from thousands of dollars of counseling), if something's going to change... something's going to have to change. It is really that simple. Truth is that many people resist change. That is, until there is a major crisis or friction. That tends to wake people up. Many times, the major change will happen after an illness, a job loss, or a catastrophe. One of my mentors, Ed Mylett says, "God doesn't do things to you, but for you". I've found that my most difficult moments have brought forth the largest changes in my life. In those moments of crisis, I could get "under it" or choose to "get after it"!

Just months before this incredible incentive trip, we were asking each other and telling ourselves it was time for a change! It felt like we were swimming upstream! We were working with a different network marketing company that provided health products. We were leading our team with passion and enthusiasm, offering solutions to our company's flailing customer service department, spending thousands of dollars on products and marketing material. In fact, we were one of the company's top recruiting distributors, personally enrolling over 200 people in our first 18 months. I was center stage at the major conferences, black-tie events, leading exercise sessions, breakout meetings, weekly webinars for the company and even shooting short testimonial videos the company would blast out via social media to use for funnel marketing.

We are loyalists. Completely committed to the mission and our team. "Look at this shiny new opportunity," has never caused us to veer off track. We easily discarded weekly messages recruiting us to the next start-up venture. We were laser focused, our feet firmly planted, ready to take on every challenge that came our way. On the outside, people thought we were at the pinnacle of success in this industry. Many thought we were earning MILLIONS. That is one of the flaws in network marketing. Many leaders live this lifestyle of never-ending positivity, or so it appears, so people want to follow them. Well like Elvis Presley said, "Truth is like the sun, it eventually shines through." Frankly, we were sick of the façade.

The truth was, financially, it was the worst and lowest income producing years since we began network marketing over 11 years ago. We were convinced things would somehow get better by working even harder. This just left us disappointed and exhausted! Another common teaching in network marketing is, "Don't quit, you're very close to your breakthrough. Winners don't quit, whiners do." Here is the truth - don't get so attached to any person, place, or thing that you give your power away or put your family in financial jeopardy. I had taken my eyes off God and made man and the "community" my idolatry. So much so, my entire family was suffering financially after we had continuously given it everything we had with that company. Two meetings a week for two years, weekly webinars, daily solutions for customer service, meeting with individuals and small groups every week. Grinding in pursuit of the "American Dream" only to feel frustrated, stressed, tired, defeated…. Proud owner of an unprofitable business.

I had lost my belief that "financial freedom" was possible with network marketing. I thought the dream was over, when it was really just beginning. I now know that God's assignment and nudging of my heart should always be priority over man's. God can guide you and move you onward and upward in your journey, if you are willing and courageous. If not, prepare to be chronically stressed and disappointed living life with a poker face. I had sacrificed "the money" for helping people or so I thought. What I KNOW for certain now, is God wants my family to have

BOTH! The heart to serve and bless others on a large scale and the opportunity to create massive wealth. We don't have to choose one or the other. It's time to wake up, if you have bought into that lie. That is not freedom - but bondage. I can help millions of people get healthy AND afford everything that my family needs along with plenty of money to serve others. I don't have to choose, unless I am choosing scarcity. I don't need to stay in my comfort zone. The "certainty" of staying where we are instead of faithfully leaping into the "unknown".

Looking back... I am so thankful we had the courage, belief and vision to make a change. That change quickly led to a massive financial breakthrough and the vacation described earlier.

As loyalists, it was difficult for us to make a change. Unfortunately, it took a family crisis to get our attention. I believe anything with your children or a loved one would do that. The crisis didn't just turn our heads, it shook us to our very core. We started to ask the right questions. We committed again to God, to each other and decided together to make the change.

CHAPTER 4

BRACE YOURSELF

Our oldest son was gearing up for winter off-season training and mentioned a small lump in his upper thigh, groin area. Expecting it to be a possible hernia we called on our friend who is an expert in his field as a local physical therapist. After close examination, it didn't appear to be a hernia and a referral was made to an oncologist. An oncologist? Why would a healthy 17-year old track athlete need to see an oncologist?

I said to myself, "Ok Lord, you have our undivided attention…"

SETBACK or SETUP?

It was the week of Christmas 2017. December 20th, 2017 to be exact. Scott informed me that I needed to take our oldest son, Beau (17) to a doctor's appointment. Sitting in the waiting room, our minds tend to wander. This is where sick people go. Why are we here? They announced our son's name. "Do you want me to go with you, Beau?"

He said, "Yeah of course, come with me mom." I was so relieved he wanted me there and that I didn't have to resort to my normal negotiations with a teenage son. I followed Beau into the examination room.

Here's a little bit about Beau. He runs like a beautiful gazelle. He's broken national track records at Hershey, PA. He has placed second at the Jr Olympics in USA Track and Field more than once. He has won more medals and ribbons than an average family with six kids in sports. Running is where he excels. He is gifted by God and he is committed to that gift with discipline. (Another principle I will discuss later.) Discipline of running when it is 30 below... Discipline of running when it is 105 on the hot track with his buddies right across the street at the pool... Discipline of daily ice baths... Discipline of running in the dark... Discipline of sacrificing family events so he could run his races. His passion is running, and everyone knows it. People love to watch him run!

There's a quick knock and the door swings open. The doctor introduces himself and begins the examination. After just a few minutes the doctor says, "Ok, you need to immediately go down for an ultrasound."

I responded, "Now? Aren't you getting ready to close?"

"Yes, but I will tell the tech to stay. It's important we do Beau's ultrasound right now."

As he was shuffling us out the door, he looked back and said, "It's definitely not a hernia. It could be lymphoma or leukemia." Thankfully Beau was about five steps ahead of me, and he did not hear those words.

My stomach was TIGHT, I was sweating, I could feel my pulse racing. We sat down in the ultrasound waiting room, and Beau looked at me and said, "Mom, what do you think it is? I am kind of nervous now as the doctor wanted the ultrasound, RIGHT NOW."

I said, "Beau, you are the healthiest young man I know. You take such excellent care of yourself. It's nothing. Good news is you don't need hernia surgery." We both laughed. I grabbed his hand and said, "Let's pray." Beau loves the Lord. He loves prayer. He loves worship music. Honestly, he is just the best young man. Not perfect but wants to course correct when he is off track. I cry as I write this. His faith is strong, and this is a total gift to my husband and me. It is one thing for your kids to "love Jesus" when they are in your home or in Sunday school. It's an entirely different thing when they "embrace their faith" as adults. To know they have faith in God is beyond powerful. It helps me to sleep better.

Suddenly, the tech appeared and said, "Hi Beau, let's get done with this so you can get out of here." I liked her positivity. I liked her upbeat attitude. I think that helped so much. Energy is contagious. Healthcare is a transference of energy. If you have ever had an ultrasound and you are looking at the screen, you feel like you are looking at alien objects. The black, white and gray are all scary if you don't know what you are looking for. So rather than look and worry, I just began to pray. The lighthearted conversation drifted from my ears and I went deep into my heart, thanking God for Beau's excellent health. I have learned to thank God in advance for the desires in your heart. This is a secret to success in all areas.

"Ok, all done," she said as she turned on the lights.

"I don't suppose you can tell me anything you saw, right?"

"That's correct, but hang tight, I will go check with the doctor and he can talk to you." Beau and I sat with anticipation, keeping our conversation light. She came back in and said, "You are free to go. The doctor will be calling you."

"Ok great, thanks so much." Beau and I were walking to the car; it was dark now. Winter in North Dakota means short, COLD days. As we slid back into the Honda, my cell phone rang. By the number, I knew it was the doctor. "Hello."

"Hello Renita. We are going to need Beau back here immediately first thing in the morning for inpatient surgery, a guided ultrasound biopsy. It's definitely not a hernia. We need to take a tissue sample right away. Please come in for outpatient surgery at 8 am tomorrow morning. You need to brace yourself. We are looking at lymphoma."

I hung up the phone. WHAT?! This was not of God. Sickness is never of God. I immediately told the devil to go back to hell. Jesus reigns in our family and in our health.

"Mom was that the doctor? What did he say?", Beau asked.

"Yep Beau, he said you need to come back in the morning for a little more testing."

"Really, mom? What do you think it is?"

"Honestly Beau, I think you are healthy. But we will come back in for the testing because he asked us to. Ok?"

Beau grabbed my hand and said, "Mom, will you pray for me again?"

"Absolutely." We thanked God for Beau's health and the amazing plan he had for Beau's life and for amazing doctors. I reminded Beau of Jeremiah 29:11 in his life, "Beau I know the plans I have for you says the Lord, plans to lift you up and prosper you; never to harm you." Beau agreed with "Amen".

CHAPTER 5

MY FIRST HIT

As soon as I got home, I started supper and the boys did homework. Beau went to his room and Scott asked how it went. "It's definitely not a hernia. We have to go back in the morning for inpatient surgery so they can do an ultrasound biopsy of those lumps."

"Really?" Scott said nervously.

"Yep, we will talk about it later," I replied.

As soon as the boys were done, and started bedtime routines, Scott and I went to our laptop computer. We googled "natural remedies for lymphoma". The first Google HIT was CBD. Every hit after was coming up with Cannabis, Marijuana, or Cannabidiol. What? Are we supposed to give our son marijuana?! Are you kidding me? My dad was a Marine and we were taught to not ever do drugs. "They'll kill you. If you do them, I'll kill you," was my dad's no-nonsense way of keeping us afraid enough to never touch them. Yikes! It worked. I have never smoked pot, not even once. (Although everyone said I should have because I am extremely fast talking and fast moving.)

As I started reading, I was blown out of the water with the amount of clinical studies done on CBD. Research kept referring to the "Endocannabinoid System (ECS)." Why didn't I know about the ECS? Most consider me an expert in health and fitness. In fact, I have been the "health and fitness expert" for 7 years on NBC's North Dakota Today show. I have a segment called, "Wellness Wednesday." Surely, I would have heard of the Endocannabinoid System, the largest self-regulatory system in the entire human body. The more Scott and I read, the more we were amazed at the thousands of studies and the powerful benefits of CBD on a broad range of health issues including many forms of cancer. In my heart, I still believed Beau didn't have ANY disease. We shut the computer and decided a better use of our time would be to pray. Not just any kind of prayers but let it all out, bawling eyes, let go of every ounce of fear kind of prayers. We did not pray with fear in our heart but stood on God's promises and the Biblical law of sowing and reaping. We had sown really amazing things into Beau's health for the past 15 years!! It was NOT for nothing. It must all add up to a healthy body. We didn't sleep that night. We prayed in faith all night, thanking God in advance for what he was doing through Beau. We thanked God for an opportunity to strengthen our faith and for humbling us so we can come to the throne yet again to seek HIM. God promises to lend His ear for those who call upon His name. We were doing just that.

When I stopped praying for a minute, my mind would drift to CBD. What the heck was that all about? I would entertain the idea for about ten seconds, "OK if something is wrong with Beau, I will give him CBD." Then I went back to praying and thanking God for Beau's healing. All of HEAVEN heard us that night.

We dropped the little brothers off at school and arrived at the hospital. Upon arrival they led us to the Oncology wing of the Hospital and to a prep room in radiology. The nurses were serious and sincere.

"Fever, ever, any fever?"

"No," Beau replied.

"Night Sweats?"

"No," Beau replied.

"Sudden weight loss?"

"Nope," Beau replied.

"Weak immune system, like have you gotten sick a lot lately?"

"No, not once. I haven't been on an anti-biotic in 13 years," Beau replied.

The nurses just looked at each other. "Well we wish you the best of luck Beau," they both said.

They wheeled him into the dark surgical room. Monitors were everywhere. Scott and I followed the rolling bed down a hallway… walking and praying for our son. In the surgical room the doctor introduced himself and immediately turned his full attention to our son.

The nurse said, "It's going to burn when we insert the needle, but it won't take long. We just need to snip a few samples of those swollen lymph nodes."

By this time, the doctor had told us that there were three swollen lymph nodes right next to each other which is typically not good. The doctor visited with Beau about track as we had just visited the University of MN, the doctor's alma mater. He spoke life over Beau talking about his track goals for the upcoming season. No doom and gloom, just optimism. Giving Beau a vision to commit to school and to commit to track. "Live with a spirit of excellence," he told Beau.

"Don't party, it's a waste of your college years. Stay focused and set yourself up for an amazing life!"

As he was talking, I thought, "Wow, this is the best speech our son could ever hear!"

In an instant, "Beau, you are done. Thanks so much for being so brave and go crush track season!"

As we exited the hospital, Beau looked at me and said, "Mom, I don't have cancer."

To which I replied, "No you don't. Your body is healthy and whole!"

CHAPTER 6

OBSESSED WITH CBD

We were told the sample tissue was to be sent away for testing and it could take five to seven days for the results to come back. In our hearts and spirits Scott and I knew Beau was healthy. We had seen so much on the first night researching CBD on the computer and eager to continue our due diligence. Over the next few days, we found ourselves reading absolutely everything we could on CBD (Cannabidiol), cannabis, and the endocannabinoid system. After we learned a little, we had an insatiable desire to learn more. Did everyone know this information except me? The stories and the research were almost miraculous. I started reaching out to my medical minded friends, nurses, doctors, etc. WOW! This is incredible. It just kept getting better and better with everything we read. I wanted our entire family to consume quality CBD. Beau first and foremost, but after reading what the endocannabinoid system does, I knew we ALL needed it, including our dog. All mammals have an endocannabinoid system.

The definition of Endocannabinoid System (ECS) from Wikipedia is:

> A biological system composed of endocannabinoids, which are endogenous lipid-based retrograde neurotransmitters that bond to cannabinoid receptors, and cannabinoid receptor proteins that are expressed throughout the mammalian central nervous system (including the brain) and peripheral nervous system. The endocannabinoid system is involved in regulating a variety of physiological and cognitive processes including fertility, pregnancy, during pre- and postnatal development, appetitive, pain-sensation, mood, and memory, and in mediating the pharmacological effects of cannabis. The ECS is also involved in mediating some of the physiological and cognitive effects of the voluntary physical exercise in humans and other animals, such as contributing to exercise-induced euphoria as well as modulating locomotor activity and motivational salience for rewards. In humans, the plasma concentration of certain endocannabinoids (i.e. anandamide) have been found to rise during physical activity, since endocannabinoids can effectively penetrate the blood brain barrier. It has been suggested that anandamide, along with other euphoria neurochemicals, contributes to the development of exercise induced euphoria in humans, a state referred to as the "runners high."

Two primary endocannabinoid receptors have

been identified. CB1, first cloned in 1990; and CB2, cloned in 1993. CB1 receptors are found predominantly in the brain and nervous system, as well as in peripheral organs and tissues, and are the main molecular target of the endocannabinoid ligand (binding molecule), anandamide, as well as its mimetic phytocannabinoid, THC. One other endocannabinoid is 2-arachidonoylglycerol (2-AG) which is active in both cannabinoid receptors, along with its own mimetic phytocannabinoid, CBD. 2-AG and CBD are involved in the regulation of appetite, immune system functions, and pain management.

They have even found CB3 receptors which are being studied with epilepsy and the build-up of proteins in the brain. More science will begin to present itself with these receptors.

To put it simply… We have "endocannabinoid receptors" throughout our entire body. The biggest concentration of receptors is found in the brain, central nervous system and the immune system. When the Endocannabinoid System of receptors are "nourished" or "fed," it helps our body regain or maintain homeostasis.

Homeostasis is simply the body maintaining internal stability. It is living in complete balance internally despite external changes. When your body is in homeostasis, it is impossible for disease to thrive.

We were praying and believing Beau's body was in

homeostasis. After all, he had no symptoms except for these swollen lymph nodes. Fortunately, we were right. On the morning of Dec 23 at 8 pm, my phone buzzed, and it was the doctor. "Renita the tests came back negative, please call me." I immediately dialed his number. It was only the second time in his medical career he went into the labs to look for himself. I asked why he felt so certain that he had cancer or a disease? He said," Just a few months ago, I had a 14-year-old boy diagnosed with Lymphoma with nearly an identical lymph node formation." I said, "Well let's not let the past predict our future. Especially with negative situations. Our faith is strong." He said, "I can see that it is." He said it is possible for those lumps to be an aggravated old injury which Beau did have in that area. Thank you, JESUS! That was the BEST CHRISTMAS present ever! Our entire family was so thankful and relieved. Our faith stood in those moments of fear and doubt. Faith isn't just positive thinking. It's being fully convinced of the thing you can't see. It's understanding both a positive or negative outcome is possible but trusting God anyway and absolutely leaning into the BEST outcome.

As our family celebrated this massive victory, the quest for the best CBD continued.

CHAPTER 7

CRISIS CREATES CLARITY

Challenges can be positive! If we have courage... It creates clarity and initiates change. I encourage you to have faith and act now!

"See I am doing a new thing! Now it springs up; do you not see it? I am making a way in the wilderness and streams in the wasteland."   Isaiah 43:19

Supporting research proves our bodies have been chronically malnourished of cannabinoids for over 80 years. For many of us, that's our entire lives. What if nourishing your body with phytocannabinoids, the kind found in hemp derived CBD, created a new path for you? What does that path look like?

I'm not claiming CBD will cure, treat or prevent disease. We are not able to say that "yet" in the United States. Go to www.echoconnection.org/education and enjoy the depth of research that has been done on CBD and a broad range of health issues. I love to click on Education to read all the studies. Do it now! Prepare to be amazed!

There are thousands of incredible studies to review. 24,000+ studies on pubmed.gov on the endocannabinoid system and cannabis. It's very encouraging to read how CBD can positively impact so many things without negative side effects that many pharmaceuticals have.

At www.echoconnection.org clinical studies support a new vision, a new path. Imagine yourself free from pain, sleeping soundly, enjoying energy and vitality. Imagine a faster fat-burning metabolism, strengthened immune system, healthy digestive system, improved memory, clarity and focus. Imagine your body working synergistically to create balance and homeostasis. Nourishing your body with CBD will be an entirely different path than most of the world is on.

Financially... Why this path? What will it look like? Projections indicate the annual amount of money spent on CBD by the year 2022 will be in excess of $22 Billion and over $57 Billion per year by 2025. If you build a CBD money tree by learning the principles introduced in this book, how will your path look drastically different from the one you're on?

CHAPTER 8

I LOVE NETWORK MARKETING

Everything that happened with Beau left Scott and I on a relentless hunt for the best quality, pure and legal CBD. After all, if we were going to consume CBD, we wanted the VERY best for our family. Coming off back to back low earning years, it would have been very easy to say let's save money and find something cheap. But after 22 years of being in health and fitness, I know with nutritional supplements, quality sometimes comes at a slightly higher price. As we continued our search for CBD, we came across many companies with several products. Finally, one company stood alone with transparency of safety, quality, testing, and the price point per mg was EXCELLENT! It's like I was getting the quality of a Mercedes Benz at a Toyota price tag! That company was Medical Marijuana Inc. We learned it was also the first publicly traded cannabis stock (MJNA) in the US stock market and actually the first company to bring non-psychoactive hemp CBD to the US from Europe. This company was the pioneer at bringing non-psychoactive CBD from hemp to the world. We dove into the information, scanning product information that could help our entire family. While scouring the information, we suddenly saw it, MJNA had a subsidiary company called Kannaway. Kannaway offered CBD products through direct sales or network marketing. I LOVE Network Marketing! This meant I wasn't forced to "only be a customer" and leave the profits to others. I could order CBD, share with others and earn money from the people I referred to Kannaway! We could get the best quality CBD on the planet while earning income by sharing these products with others who absolutely need them!

My passion was reignited. I felt in that moment, the entire experience with Beau was a "God assignment" to realign me. I had found the CBD I wanted my family to consume and somehow by the grace of God, stumbled across the business of the 21st Century! There are lots of different ways to make money with CBD. Let's cut to the chase. A system with a proven and predictable pattern of activities will save us time and maximize our profits. That is what we wanted to create incredible momentum and massive income. I love health and helping people change their lives. It becomes a lot more fun when you are earning amazing income by referring and leading others with the absolute best products!

We knew from previous experience, it's important to be a "product of the product." We wanted to taste, touch and see all that Kannaway had to offer. Based on our massive financial goals, we invested in the Total Product Experience Value Pack for $1,999. We didn't hesitate in fear. We didn't wrestle with indecision. We KNEW with certainty these Kannaway CBD products would help our family. CBD will help every family. Our vision was clear, and it was time to get to work! That's exactly what we did next. We were excited to help one million people nourish their Endocannabinoid Systems and create massive wealth doing it!

CHAPTER 9

SHOW ME THE MONEY

I was thrilled but nervous to announce I had enrolled with the BEST hemp-derived CBD company on the planet. I called my sponsor, Randy 3 times in one day and asked him, "Are you sure I am not going to get arrested?" I knew we were federally legal in all 50 states because our hemp was harvested from Europe but there was a tremendous amount of confusion in the marketplace. At that time (Dec 20, 2017), the Farm Bill had not yet been signed and I wasn't 100% positive how people would react. I knew with CERTAINTY that it was a divine appointment, so I was confident God had my back. "How do I make money the fastest?" was my next question.

He said, "You need to sponsor 3 people with the value packs. They can be customers or brand ambassadors. When you do that in the first 30 days, you will receive FAST START bonuses which means TRIPLE Direct

Sales Commissions for the life of your business. That meant $60 instead of $20, $225 instead of $75, $300 instead of $100 and $450 instead of $150. I was definitely going to go Fast Start immediately to max out the comp plan!

My sponsor said, "Renita, you need to follow the 10 steps to success. If you follow all 10, you will have success. If you do 5 of them, you won't. Can I set a time to do a New Member Orientation with you to discuss them?"

"Yes, in the meantime, I need to make money. I am going to start enrolling. I know I have 30 days, but I will go FAST START today!" I said.

I think many "home based business" owners come from a "mindset" of product sales. We believe in a product, so we talk about it. I didn't want to wait to get my product to start talking about the Endocannabinoid System (ECS) and how CBD could help. This is the "information age" and people are always looking for things that work better. I wanted to be FIRST talking about it on Facebook. If I didn't know the difference between hemp and marijuana, I was sure the majority didn't either. I knew a secret the world hadn't discovered yet. I was eager to share. "To whom much is given, much is expected." - Luke 12:48

Everyone has an opinion on "social media," some good and some bad. In life, I believe most are seeking improvement and open to suggestions. A mentor taught me to look at people's lives and ask myself if I want ANY area of my life to look like theirs; physically, financially, relationally, mentally, or spiritually. If the answer is NO, don't follow their lead. If the lifestyle they're living aligns with YOUR values and the direction you want to move, listen to their advice. The challenge with success in "health," "wealth creation," "relationships," and "faith" is we allow imposters to speak into our lives. Be careful who you let speak into your heart. Your mind is the watchdog for your heart. When launching your business, protect your heart. Be careful whose advice you take. It takes time to filter those people out on social media, but I did it. Character is eventually revealed in every situation.

In this chapter of my life, I wanted to do more than "sell a product." Honestly, how many "product salespeople" do you know that are living the life of their dreams? Car salesman, magazine salesman, book salesman, and clothing salesman; most are trading hours for dollars. If they're earning a great income, it's usually because they're putting in 80+ hour work weeks and sacrificing other areas of their lives. I was ready to make a huge impact with people's health and create massive wealth!

I envisioned a mega-team of passionate servant leaders running towards financial freedom. 21st Century businessmen and women working from homes, phones, computers, and online sources. I dreamt of what financial freedom would feel like with our family. To have abundance physically AND financially. Network marketing has taught me to dream big and work hard. The only limits are the ones in your mind. Although we drop our kids off at school and pick them up together every day, I longed for more. NO more financial stress. NO more money arguments about bills. I wanted to teach our boys to be entrepreneurs and show them how to set a goal, work smart and hard. I wanted to not only create health, wealth and life freedom for our family but to help every other family that wanted it. In addition, Scott and I wanted to help our aging parents. We were ready for a financial blessing!

Are you:

Ready to get outside of your comfort zone?

Tired of the status quo?

Sick of being strapped financially?

Ready to improve your health and the health of your family?

Wanting to make an impact in your community, country, and world?

I still believe in the power of the human spirit to desire more and then do something about it! Do you desire to raise your children instead of putting them in daycare from 7 am - 6 pm? Honestly, who is supposed to be watching, loving, teaching, feeding, and potty training your kids? I choose to max out, raise up champions, travel the world, retire early, help my aging parents, all while changing millions of lives. Why not? Our God is a big God and we don't have to sink to a half-hearted, lack luster vision of complacency and depression. Forget it! I am determined to live out the 3:20 life on Earth! "Now to him who is able to do immeasurably more than all we ask or imagine, according to His power that is at work within us."- Ephesians 3:20.

A SYSTEM is created to Save Your Self Time, Energy, and Money. Just think of every successful franchise, church, education model, weight loss system, sports team, online funnel and everything else that is "WORKING." Smart entrepreneurs realize this quickly and implement a system instead of wasting time. Unless you have time to waste, I would encourage you to find a system that works and get to work on maxing it out!

I LOVE creativity. Truth is, I want to be financially free FASTER so that I can put my creativity to work. That happens by following a SYSTEM. When you have more money, you have more options. It's really that simple. There IS room for creativity while building your CBD MONEY TREE, but the truth is, do The 10 Steps to Success FIRST. If you implement the proven SYSTEM, you can do anything above and beyond to build your business. "Is what I am doing duplicatable?" is the real question. The magic in network marketing is... Duplicate, duplicate, duplicate. If you can show someone the tools within the system and they use them to build their business, you have discovered the magic of network marketing. Sometimes creativity alone leads to little or NO MONEY. Lots of great ideas and no implementation leads to massive frustration. There are a lot of creative broke people. You can be creative and create massive wealth by following a SYSTEM.

Allow me to share another family story. My parents are some of the hardest workers you'll ever meet. Although they worked hard, we were not wealthy. I would say we were middle class. Growing up, I did not live in a state of financial freedom. Money was a stressor in our home. To put it plainly, we were a hard-working middle-class family who never slowed down enough to break out of that lifestyle. Like Ed Mylett says, "Middle class is the toughest class to break out of." I am determined to be a chain breaker. When we know better, we get to do better. I don't have to live in a state of financial struggle or work 100+ hours a week. If you can identify a generational curse, stop it. You have the power. I know "abundance" is the truth of how God wants us to live. I believe for a life of prosperity and health for our family and every generation after.

My parents worked HARD but not necessarily SMART. Dad was ravaged with resentment of a job he hated coupled with alcohol addiction which never leads to financial abundance. Mom was a hard worker that created a large menu of German comfort food at her restaurant. It was her passion. Unfortunately, her passion in the kitchen left her barely getting by financially and leaky gut syndrome. The menu was too complex, and employees were stealing from her. There wasn't a system in place for cutting expenses, optimizing talent, and increasing revenue.

My brothers are both tremendously successful in business. One of my brothers owns about a dozen franchises. He follows the systems precisely that are part of his franchise. As a result, he creates massive wealth. The freedom that wealth provides allows him to implement creative ideas in his life and family. Following a SYSTEM is crucial to maxout your time and money.

The great news about Kannaway is you don't have to pay a $50,000 franchise free and you don't need to invest in a $250,000 buildout to start. You don't have to manage employees, which is sometimes like adult daycare.

Kannaway has a proven system to create incredible results. The startup is low and success is not determined by just your own efforts. You have a team of business partners passionate about creating a difference in this world! I decided to join the mission to share CBD with others and create wealth with Kannaway! Are you ready to do the same?

CHAPTER 10

DUPLICATE THE NEW MEMBER ORIENTATION

"Let's do that new member orientation", I said to my sponsor. "If that's the SYSTEM, train me so I can run with it!" The new member orientation consists of the 10 steps to success. Learning this and implementing these steps will be crucial to your business. Remember, by implementing 3 of the 10, you will not experience financial freedom. By implementing 7 of the 10, your financial dreams will not occur. WILLINGNESS and IMPLEMENTATION of all 10 steps creates duplication and the "magic seeds" for a CBD money tree begin to take root. Activate the SYSTEM daily (water your CBD money tree) until you reach your desired outcome. This is foundational for your financial success!

Consistent massive action with a system is foundational for financial success.

Is your goal to earn free CBD product and a few extra hundred dollars a month? Do you want to make a few thousand dollars a month? Some of you reading this will say, "I have a millionaire and beyond mindset." That is fantastic! Your vision will expand while you are on the journey. I believe if God gave us the vision all at once, it would blow our minds! You may not have the million-dollar mindset when you begin, but as your journey continues, the path becomes clear. As you continue to work in the CBD space, you will realize how many people are looking for safe, quality, effective CBD. As you work through the Kannaway ranks, the path to greater success becomes evident. I have realized growth-minded, goal-oriented people are always stretching, growing, and wanting more. Being a little competitive doesn't hurt either.

Many times, I hear people say, "just be content." Being thankful for what the good Lord has blessed us with is so important. In the same breath, our God is a BIG GOD. In some of His children, He puts big desires to help millions of people and make millions of dollars.

Arguing about finances is never God's heart for our homes. Marriages ending because of financial difficulty is a major problem. We need to take action in courage. We need to teach "finances" in our faith walk. Our family unit should understand how to earn, save, invest, multiply, and tithe. He wants His children to grow and become more like Heaven on Earth... Think ABUNDANCE! Money put in the hands of people with great hearts can help heal the planet.

CHAPTER ELEVEN

DUPLICATION = MULTIPLICATION

The right company/products/timing with a proven SYSTEM will put you in a position to win financially. I have been with a great company who had good products but no SYSTEM. This led to financial frustration. You need fantastic products, a proven SYSTEM and an insatiable work ethic to capitalize. Some companies have average products and people are winning financially. The fact that we have the absolute safest, highest quality, most efficacious products on the planet with Kannaway is a blessing. With the end of the prohibition of cannabis, we weren't looking to earn a little income. The timing, products, and opportunity is a financial game changer for those who take full advantage of it!

Let's discuss the 10-Steps to Success.

This proven and predictable system is also available

digitally in your back office and on your Kannaway Connect app once you are signed up as a Brand Ambassador.

#1 WHY Do You Want to Build a Kannaway Business?

Determine your WHY and then immediately figure out your emotional and mental barrier of exit.

I used to hear, "If your why makes you cry" then you will succeed in your business." Many times, this is true as tears demonstrate an "emotional connection". The deeper the emotion, the stronger the conviction and commitment to the path.

Have you heard of the pain/pleasure principle? Very few people are motivated by "pleasure" when it comes to making a major lifestyle change. Consider health and weight loss. If you eat on the PFC Plate (a super cool tool I created to help you turn on your metabolisms and nourish your body found at www.pfcplate.com) and exercise daily, you will experience excellent health. Look around… How many people do? Instead people chronically diet. They wait until they have a health crisis. They are addicted to suffering, clinging to emotional baggage, food, drama, and the past.

Another example is marriage. If you consistently apply honor and respect you will have a great marriage. How many flourishing marriages do you see? Instead we see more than half of marriages ending in divorce. The solutions seem simple, but most will tell you "change is hard". That is until there is a crisis.

I have found out what is highly effective in 23 years of being a lifestyle coach. People generally change when they are in a high trauma situation. That is… If they live through it. Change occurs more rapidly when people are in pain and their backs are up against a wall. Basically, major transformation occurs when the SH!T hits the fan! Or at least the decision to transform happens at that moment. You can decide to change in an instant. When you do, it immediately changes your chemistry. You live through the heart attack and are ready to get healthy. You lose your job and are ready to start that business you have always dreamed of. Because of the "life interrupt", you have disrupted your mental patterns. You are now committed to living with different actions. Those new daily choices become habits and will change your brain and your life. After 21 days, you create new neuropathy (neurogenesis). You moved from stinkin' thinkin' to a highway of possibility. Think of it like new, healthier routes for your brain. The longer you can apply those actions or habits, the stronger your chance of long-term change will be.

Habits create results; good and bad. If you want to change your life, change your habits! Remember this… YOU DON'T HAVE TO WAIT FOR A CRISIS TO CHANGE. You just need to **decide** and **commit.** This principle has helped me tremendously. I have chosen to become excellent at changing because I want to, not because I have to. Say it out loud, "I GET TO CHANGE! I LOVE TO GROW!" "Get to" instead of "have to" will change your mind, your emotions, and your life. It makes change enjoyable! I consider it to be a great adventure!

When the pain of staying the same becomes greater than the pain of change, you will grow.

Remember, crisis is a huge motivator- while you are experiencing it. It moves you out of complacency immediately. Most likely, you are forced to make the decision. Crisis helped lead us to Kannaway. Once we realized what we had our hands on, we committed and there was no turning back. It was one of the best financial decisions of our lives!

Determine "why" you want to do this. Write it down and own it. Does it captivate you emotionally and mentally? Are you desperate? Are you passionate? Does it make you want to fly out of the bed in the morning? A ho-hum "why" will result in nothing changing. It has to be deep. Go all in! Quantify your why. Then tell it to someone you love who believes in you. Don't tell it to the "dream crushers." Tell it to the ultimate "dream giver... GOD. As soon as you voice it, your life will begin to shift. The Reticular Activation System (RAS) of your brain takes over. Your RAS starts looking for ways to make it happen! You have just opened your mind up to abundance and possibility versus depravation and negativity.

Now that you have your "why," it's time to determine your emotional and mental barrier of exit. Basically, that is a fancy way of saying, "I WILL NEVER QUIT" when the going gets tough. Being an entrepreneur means weathering peaks and valleys without losing enthusiasm. Are you capable of getting your emotions under control when the stress hits? Most people are ruled by their emotions. They usually have a difficult time having huge financial success as an entrepreneur. Keep in mind being "emotionally reactive" is much different than being "passionate". Passion is powerful in the marketplace. It's like a magnet as most people are living half asleep. This is probably because they aren't getting great quality of sleep at night, which again, our CBD may help with.

Keep in mind as you launch your business, some people are still ignorant and fearful of network marketing. Be prepared for ignorance, fear, doubt, shame, and people inflicting their "limited beliefs" on you. When these interactions inevitably occur, will you be prepared? If you are committed to your "why" and will not quit based on somebody else's opinion, you will do well in this business. I quit listening to people talk negatively about network marketing when I realized four things: 1. They have never had any success with network marketing because they have been closed minded. 2. They jumped from company to company and now nobody trusts them. They could still have success if they would decide to commit and rebuild their trust. 3. They didn't have the financial success I was looking for, so their opinion was pointless. 4. They hadn't offered to pay my bills so their negative opinion about how I was going to create wealth was meaningless to me.

My favorite word when prospecting is NEXT!

God's already aligned my team; I must go find them.

Your emotional and mental barrier will keep you in the game when dealing with tough people and situations. It will keep you from quitting on your dreams, even on your worst day.

Our why along with our mental and emotional barrier of exit is our family. Living out our best life here on earth so we can inspire and serve others. Our 3 boys are watching and learning what commitment and integrity is. We are also committed to our extended family and friends whose lives have changed because of Kannaway. Our team members who have shared their goals with us and the promises we've made to each other. It's all the dreams we have heard and encouraged. We choose not to quit. Because it wouldn't just be quitting a business. It would be giving up on our dreams and dreams of people we love and care about. We care deeply about this and partner with our team to work towards their success. We love helping restore hope to the hopeless. We love showing families how to regain health and wealth which ultimately leads to more freedom.

Look back for an instant as you prepare to press forward. Do you have children? In our first network marketing business we lived in a neighborhood with 10 sex offenders living within a 4-block radius. I never felt comfortable letting the boys out to shoot hoops without us sitting right next to them. We desperately wanted out to have FREEDOM with our boys. I hated that feeling of always looking over my shoulder when unloading groceries in my driveway. We wanted a house like the one described in the song BIG HOUSE. "A big, big house, with lots and lots of rooms, a big, big table with lots and lots of food, a big, big yard, where we can play football! That's my Father's house!" For those of you who don't know that AUDIO ADRENALINE song… Go listen to it. Sometimes a song gives you a vision of what is possible. We realized THAT is the house we wanted for our boys. We weren't about to apologize for wanting more. We were going to go for it. Within one year, we were out of that rat-infested neighborhood and living in a cul-de-sac in a 4600 square foot house. It is all about getting a vision and then going for it!

Maybe its college tuition. Maybe it's a family vacation. Maybe you want to save lives with this incredible plant. Maybe it is because you want to be part of the end of the prohibition of cannabis. Maybe it's a house. Maybe it's your aging mom's teeth, which is now on my list as well. I just want the ability to say, "Mom go get whatever you need done at the dentist, and send me the bill." That is definitely motivating for Scott and I with our aging parents. "Pearl's teeth… Sometimes we just want to be able to pay for teeth." If you have a family and are also helping with aging parents, you get my drift. We never have to apologize or explain to someone the desires of our heart. God put the desires there to serve others. Especially if those desires are for love, generosity, goodness, safety, health, and vitality of others.

This is our integrity. God first, family next. We trust and have faith in God's plan for our lives. We don't give up on family. We have promised our boys time freedom to attend everything they are involved in. To help them achieve their dreams. We have promised them unlimited opportunity if God is calling them to an area. That takes time, energy, and money. We want incredible wealth but not at the cost of our family time, which we see so many times in entrepreneurship. In addition, we have promised our teams that this incredible way of creating wealth truly works, if they are consistent and persistent. Our SYSTEM and INCREDIBLE products are changing lives physically and financially. We will not quit on them. In return, we ask that they do not quit on their dreams. This is a special opportunity. It's not lonely at the top of the mountain when you are standing with all your friends and family. It's shared success. Teamwork makes the dream work!

Onward and upward!

Going back to a job where I know everyone is replaceable is a mental and emotional barrier of exit for me. In my weakest, hardest moments I think "I will never quit!" If I would, then what? Go back to a job where my earnings are limited, and my time is controlled? Go back to a job where my boss doesn't value and honor me? Look around. Do your coworkers hate their jobs, their lives, and their spouse? A recent study showed that nearly 80% of people in the US hate their jobs and would rather be doing something else. Is this why so many are getting on depression, anxiety, and sleeping medication? Status quo has got to go!!! Suicide rate is up 33%. Tragically in 2017 there was an estimated 1.4 million suicide attempts in the United States. People are unhappy. Think about going back to a JOB? NO THANKS!! I do not want that for my life or yours! WAKE UP… The pursuit for the "American dream" was never meant to be a NIGHTMARE. I am so thankful. Even on my toughest day, I will take a little more CBD, pray, exercise, breathe deeply, go do something FUN and revisit my Kannaway business first thing in the morning. A good night's rest changes perspective.

Imagine vivid, descriptive specifics to what it is that you want. Write it out. On paper, on your bathroom mirror, in your closet, in your car, and everywhere you spend time. People who are specific and write down their goals reach their goals more often compared to those who don't. The reason is two part. First part is external storage and second part is neuroscience. External storage is the tangible part where you are recording something in a visual place where you can revisit it OFTEN. Your eyes are the gate to your soul. I write my goals down in places like on my bathroom mirror in bright red lipstick, notebooks, and posted notes throughout our home. Trust me, red lipstick is NOT easy to get off the bathroom mirror, which again helps you from starting and stopping a bunch of things. In addition, you read it out loud every time you stand in front of the mirror, which is where neuroscience comes in. Laying down new routes. New neural pathways. It is a healthy brain washing every time you read your goals out loud.

In the science world, it is called encoding. Encoding is the biological process by which the things we perceive travel to our brain's hippocampus where they are analyzed. From there, decisions are made about what gets stored in our long-term memory and in turn what gets discarded. Writing improves that encoding process. So basically, when you write things down, they have a much greater chance of being remembered. Plus, studies show individuals demonstrate better memory for material they have written down vs material they have read. I think of it as laying down NEW neural pathways (a new route for your brain). But remember, it's not one and done. It must be revisited often times a day for a minimum of 21 days for it to become a NEW pattern of thinking. It may be time to build a new road instead of the highway to hell you've been on. If something is working and improving your entire life, why stop at 21 days? By then, a new positive habit has been created and success is obtained much easier! Keep going!!

Step One - Success Questions:

1.   WHY do you want to launch your CBD business?
2.   WHAT is your emotional and mental barrier of exit?
3.   WHO did you tell that loves you and believes in you?
4.   WHEN will you commit, plant seeds and water your CBD money tree?
5.   WHERE did you write down your specific goals?

Now shut your eyes and visualize yourself succeeding. Breathe it in. Deeply.

#2 Place an Appropriate First Order

Based on our goal and what was financially appropriate for us, we chose to get started with the Kannaway Total Product Experience Pack. It was the best decision as we wanted to maxout our income and genuinely represent all of Kannaway's amazing products. We understood the importance of an "appropriate first order."

In the big picture of your business, to invest $1,999 an amount that with effort is easy to cashflow… is just a drop in the bucket. Many franchises and traditional businesses cost hundreds of thousands or more. The average franchise fee today is roughly $50,000. Depending on the business you could be looking at a $250,000+ build out for a location. You're down $300,000+ and you should expect to work 50-80 hours per week for the next 2-5 years before paying back, breaking even and earning your first $1 profit. $1999 is really a small but powerful investment to build a global million-dollar business…if you are willing to do the work!

Step Two - Success Questions:

1. What are my financial goals with this business?
2. Will experiencing a variety of Kannaway's products help me reach my financial goals?
3. What is financially appropriate for me to launch my business?

4. Am I willing to do the work necessary to succeed?

Consider your goals and business strategy when placing your initial order. We chose to MAXOUT the compensation plan. The real question is, WILL YOU? Our success strategy is to educate the world about Kannaway, the global cannabis leader, hemp, CBD, terpenes and the Endogenous Cannabinoid System (ECS), to provide products that support that message, and to implement the absolute BEST SYSTEM for duplication of leadership and wealth creation.

Placing your initial order of a Jr. Executive Pack, Sr. Executive Pack, or Total Product Experience Pack (like we did) will supply you with a variety of incredible products! It will give you enough supply to share with others for the business-building activities you'll undergo. You will touch, taste and feel all that Kannaway has to offer. Plus, by placing the appropriate order of one of the business builders' packs, you will maxout the compensation plan (think triple direct sales commissions). You might as well earn triple commissions on value packs purchased by your new brand ambassadors and customers, right? Our products are truly life changing and superior to anything else we have seen in the marketplace. Safety, purity, quality, triple lab testing, Certificates of

Analysis, CO_2 extraction, only CBD in the PDR listing, QR Codes on every product to take you directly to labs, and legality DEFINITELY matter in the marketplace.

It's your CBD MONEY TREE!

The three Fast Start value packs include the Fast Start Jr Executive Pack ($699), the Fast Start Sr Executive Pack ($899) and the Fast Start Total Product Experience Pack ($1999). Which "fast start" value pack will you launch your business with and why?

#3 Set up Monthly Smartship

Smartship is the lifeblood of your online business. You can choose any of the products totaling 110 PV. It is important for several reasons but the biggest reason from a business standpoint is you must maintain 110 PV (personal volume) or greater to maxout the compensation plan and receive all bonuses Kannaway has to offer. We don't want anyone leaving any money on the table because they forgot to set up their smartship. We had a few team members miss out on $1000 bonuses because they forgot to enroll on smartship. That was a tough lesson.

Remember ALL 10 STEPS will lead you to financial freedom. Your team builders will duplicate what you do, so set the standard and set up smartship immediately. You can always change what you are receiving each month.

From a health consumer standpoint, there are two reasons smartship is truly SMART:

Consistency - People who are consistent with their health

habits experience the greatest results. As you know eating healthy occasionally will never create the body of your dreams. The benefits of CBD vary per individual but will be positively undeniable for most. When the body regains homeostasis, your entire life changes for the better. We can help balance our hormones, get rid of brain-fog, sleep soundly with no more racing mind or wild kicking at night, increase energy, feel better and smile more. Who doesn't want to be more happy more often?

Convenience - Products shipped to your doorstep makes life easier. As a society, we are busy, lazy, technologically confused, or can simply forget to reorder something as amazing as CBD! Scheduling smartship gives you peace of mind and is a real blessing. If people forget smartship, they call you in a panic after they have been out for a few days because their sleeping is back on the crazy train.

Smartship allows your business to flow smoothly by consistently providing the product your business requires, while greatly cutting down on the time spent on administrative tasks. Enroll with Kannaway's best value smartship packages or any products you love and want to enjoy. Smartship is what you want to personally consume and have on hand to share with others. It's your only fixed business expense.

A powerful way to support your downline/team is to teach them how to create exponential growth and financial breakthrough. Committing to smartship and teaching your leaders to do the same will create financial success.

Step Three - Success Questions:

1. Are you ready for better health and wealth?
2. Did you set up your Monthly Smart Ship?
3. Was it 110 personal volume (pv) or more so you can maxout Kannaway's compensation plan?
4. Will you teach your team the importance of smartship?

#4 Review All Resources in Kannaway Backoffice/Kannaway Connect app

Did you go to High School? Did you go to college? Did you have any training when you started a new job? Maybe some of you went to several weeks of training or read a manual before you began. Truth is STEP #4 is like your high school and college education. Difference is, most of you had to go through 12 to 20 years of school and earn a degree before you earned a dollar in that field. Statistics show that most entrepreneurs work at least 5 years before breaking even. That is crazy! Who has that much time to waste being broke and stressed before earning a $1 profit? Building your CBD MONEY TREE allows you to cash flow your business start-up and monthly expenses quickly. In our case… We cash flowed our start-up before our first order even arrived!

Reviewing the amazing resources in your online Kannaway account and Kannaway Connect app will EMPOWER YOU and STRENGTHEN YOUR ABILITY TO ACT QUICKLY and CORRECTLY! Incredible tools are at your fingertips. Logging in to your Kannaway online back-office, you will find phenomenal visual, audio, training, and printable resources. By clicking on business and marketing materials, you will have hundreds of powerful resources at your fingertips. The Kannaway Connect app is super simple to use and duplicatable with your team. The great news is you don't have to "know it all" to begin. You just have to know which tool to point to. Part of your leadership development will be the rate at which you learn and how quickly you take action! You are in the driver's seat. Go at the speed you desire. How fast do you want to reach your goals? You don't have to know it all to start. The skill to do comes from the doing! Remember, the tools will do the talking in this business. Either you utilize a tool, or you become a tool (haha)!

The CBD MONEY TREE, Kannaway online back-office materials, Kannaway Connect app, Kway Global FaceBook group, www.echoconnection.org , weekly Wednesday Kannaway corporate webinars, and weekly Mastermind group sessions are tools that will help you start and grow your business successfully. To the extent you learn to leverage these tools and teach others to do the same, your business will grow. Consistent review will strengthen and develop you as a leader. You can only teach what you have experienced. Get in there and learn to experience it all.

Step Four - Success Questions:

1. Are you coachable?
2. Do you want to grow as a leader so you can help others grow?
3. Do you want to use the tools or be a tool?
4. How quickly will you learn from these resources and duplicate yourself by training your team?

#5 Build Belief

Have you ever heard the saying, "WHAT WERE YOU THINKING?" This is where it's going to get deep. Just like an oak tree with a strong root system, we must go deep to grow something that will last. If we don't go there we can't grow to soaring heights personally and financially.

OUR THOUGHTS CREATE OUR BELIEFS

OUR BELIEFS GOVERN OUR ACTIONS

OUR ACTIONS BECOME HABITS

OUR HABITS BUILD OUR CHARACTER

OUR CHARACTER FORMS OUR DESTINY

When you make the powerful conscious decision to focus on your thoughts and direct your attention correctly, you can actually change physical matter. Your brain, hormones, mood, and body change in a healthy way.

Stop... breathe... Please re-read the previous paragraph!

Catch your thoughts on purpose! Engage your brain's sensory processing and rewiring systems. Stimulate your neurotransmitters, your genetic expression, and even your cellular activity in a positive direction! Think about what you're thinking about! Thoughts that fire together wire together. The great news is WE GET TO CHOOSE our thoughts. You rule them. They should NOT be controlling you.

Now let's get to your beliefs. Beliefs are at the root of each choice you make and ultimately who you are. What do YOU believe?

Belief is the catalyst of all people. It literally governs everything in your life. Every decision you make is an outward demonstration of your belief. Examine your own life. You are consciously and unconsciously living out your beliefs every single day... Good or bad. What do you believe about health? You are living that out. What do you believe about eating healthy? You are living that out. What do you believe about money? You are living that out.

To grow a successful CBD MONEY TREE, you must develop the correct beliefs while ridding your mind, emotions and life of the wrong beliefs. This is a process, but one worth the undertaking. How much is it worth? It's worth millions! What will you do with those millions? Start asking yourself that question.

Belief is not just a mental state. Usually it begins with a strong emotional situation. We let it enter our hearts which is where it becomes rooted. High emotional experiences are the ones we remember because it went from our head to our heart. Or did it go from our heart to our head? In many cases, beliefs happen in our childhood without any understanding of what was occurring. Think about an example. You were a small child and you witnessed your parents intensely arguing about money. You listened and immediately it penetrated your heart. You were scared and began crying. You did not feel safe and secure. This created a belief. The belief planted a tree (neural pathway). The fruit of the tree says, "there is not enough money" or "strife is attached to money." Usually every belief we have can connect back to an emotional experience. That is why it is so CRUCIAL that we be watchdogs for our hearts. If you hear something, ask yourself, "Is it God's truth?" Is it a "limited belief of someone else?" Is it from someone who has never monitored their heart-mind connection? Do not take everything to heart... Especially the crap, negativity, and opinions of others. Be specific about guarding your heart and any negative intake when it comes to growing your CBD MONEY TREE.

Ask yourself if what you are reading and listening to is developing your character and growing your business. If it's not, cut it loose. Just think, if 10 people were given $100 and told to spend it wisely. All 10 would do different things with that money. Some of those activities may NOT be wise in our mind. Their beliefs were the difference maker! Beliefs determine how they spent, invested, or buried that money. Actions follow belief.

In network marketing you can earn millions of dollars if you follow the proven and predictable SYSTEM. Your actions and the decisions you make are based on your beliefs. Your beliefs are up to you! Your beliefs will help you rule or make you a fool. YOU DECIDE WHAT THOUGHTS YOU HAVE. YOU DECIDE WHAT YOU BELIEVE. YOU DECIDE YOUR SUCCESS!

Do everything in your power and the power (Holy Spirit) living in you to do 3 things.

1. Examine/identify your personal beliefs. What do you believe about yourself? What do you believe about God? What do you believe about money? What do you believe about your potential? What do you believe you are worth? Beliefs become a self-fulfilling prophecy in our lives. Are these beliefs creating the life you desire? We must always

be aware of our beliefs and guard our hearts at all cost.

2. <u>Be willing to "give up," "cut loose," and "throw off"</u>
<u>any belief that is hindering your growth.</u> It's time to prune
the tree. When you consciously remove these negative
thoughts from your life, you will be able to disconnect
and desynchronize the neurons. If they stop firing
together, they will no longer wire together. Some of these
may be hard to leave behind. A few examples of deep-
rooted beliefs include, "It's how I was raised," or "I've
always been this way." The only question I have for you
is, "How is that working for you?" Have courage and
faith to remove any negative and limited beliefs.

3. <u>Plant the correct new beliefs.</u> You're building a new
tree (neural pathway)! When we begin to do this our
bodies begin to release certain chemicals like oxytocin,
dopamine, and serotonin which increase feelings of love,
peace and happiness. This powerful conscious decision
changes harmful brain activity into healthy new and
positive pathways in our brain. You can make the
decision in an instant. Then it's important to ACTIVATE
these new thoughts every day until the new belief is
formed. This is called neuroplasticity of the brain. It
literally grows new brain trees when we start believing
and thinking positive. The trees grow stronger and bigger
every day. Think of an oak tree! Stay in that thought
pattern and eventually that old "wiring" will be
COMPLETELY GONE. You will no longer feel stuck.
The choice is yours. You can choose to keep thinking the
same or change it. Either way, protein synthesis occurs. A
toxic memory can be eliminated. The choice is ultimately
up to each one of us. I love to align my thoughts with the
Word of God, as the Bible was the most powerful book

ever written. Each word is true and inspired by God. God doesn't put limits on us to do great things. We put them on ourselves. He is an UNLIMITED Father. It's time to break every chain and activate the power of the Holy Spirit to change our brain and ultimately our lives. I love and recommend the books "Switch on Your Brain" by Dr. Caroline Leaf and "Breaking the Habit of Being Yourself" by Dr. Joe Dispenza.

Here is the truth that you can take to heart about Kannaway. Kannaway's leadership is experiencing tremendous success. You can join in and share these results by strengthening these four key beliefs.

1. Network Marketing has many advantages over conventional business.
2. Kannaway is an excellent company with tremendous products.
3. Kannaway provides an experienced and effective leadership team.
4. You will succeed when you follow the system of Kannaway's "10 Steps to Success."

Belief in network marketing /direct selling occurs by studying the industry. We read the book "Business of the 21st Century" by Robert Kiyosaki. This single book shifted our lives many years ago. We read it several times and knew we wanted to be in this wealth accumulating industry. We learned why network marketing is the "Business of the 21st Century." We decided to become "Conscientious Capitalists". We're not looking to win at the demise or cost of others. We're looking to win as we lead others in winning and by improving lives and health of our planet. That has always been on our hearts and a major priority for our family. "Go Pro" by Eric Worre is another great educational tool for building belief in network marketing. It helps you to overcome obstacles on the journey.

Building belief in the product happens by consistently consuming Kannaway's products and sharing with others. Once you're involved, you'll witness everyone raving about how amazing they feel. People ask me which products I use. We use all of them! Our family (including our dog) enjoys every one of Kannaway's amazing products. We continue to be fascinated by the articles and clinical studies posted at www.echoconnection.org. Reviewing this information strengthens our belief in CBD and its incredible healing potential. It reinforces our decision to consume CBD daily as a family.

It's been easy to believe in Kannaway's leadership. They are true pioneers and have remarkable character in business. Dr. Stuart Titus, Blake Schroeder, Brad Tayles, Randy Schroeder, Dr. Janelle Kim, Stephen Jones, Alex Grapov, Justin Stephens, Chris Mahlmann Andrea Barnes, and many others… these individuals are servant leaders. Be sure to log in to Kannaway's weekly Wednesday webcasts for continued information and training. Most importantly, get to a large Kannaway event where you can personally meet Kannaway leaders and the Echoconnection families. One event will change your life!

#6 Create Your Initial Candidate List

This step is crucial and so very valuable. When I first started planting my CBD MONEY TREE, I challenged myself to write down at least 100 names of people I wanted to share with. I am constantly adding to my list each day. This task is easy and fun. Most of our phones store 300+ contacts. Facebook, Instagram, and other social media outlets store another 400+ friends. The best thing is each of those friends has 400+ friends of their own. It is an infinite forest of money trees, waiting to be planted!

Take a one-minute break right now.

We are going to have a one-minute CBD brainstorm session. Write down every name you can think of. Set the timer on your phone for 1 minute. Ready, set, go! Action is KEY to this business. Write down the name of every single person you know without prejudging them. That can be tricky. Our past dictates limited beliefs many times. Let it go, people change. Situations change people. Life changes people. Don't skip a name because, "She's not the sales type," and "He makes too much money," and "He'd never be interested in this," or "I don't have the courage to talk to her." Simply write down the name of every person you know. On your list, there could be one or two people with the potential to reach the highest rank as Kannaway Brand Ambassadors. There are also 20 or 30 people who are not looking for a business opportunity now but want to use our products as a customer. We don't know which path they will choose. You might be surprised at who decides to take advantage of this opportunity.

If you run out of people, no worries. In your Kannaway Connect app and Kannaway back office under "Business" you will find the 10 steps to success in which you will find a candidate memory jogger. Don't make the classic mistake of thinking about 5 or 6 people you think will be interested and stopping there. Make sure you write down at least 100 names. Keep in mind, one person's opinion or decision should not have any negative effect on your business. Remember, some people function from those toxic memory trees! Many people think and act from their limited beliefs! Remember, you are learning to grow new trees, both in your mind and your CBD MONEY TREE!

#7 Learn to Invite

Invite people to a KANNAWAY EVENT! It is foundational to the growth of your CBD MONEY TREE. We also utilize the following: Facebook Live watch parties, Zoom, GoToMeetings or you could grow your business by meeting people in person. That choice is completely up to you. We do a combination of all the above to build our business.

The invitation is very simple. These two questions have proven to be successful in engaging discussion and confirming guests.

1. "What have you heard about the health benefits of CBD?" This question is product focused and gets people engaged in conversation with you.

2. "What have you heard about the CBD financial opportunity called the GREEN-RUSH?" This question is opportunity focused and creates discussion relating to business.

Ask and then listen. Let people talk. Everyone has an opinion. Remember, opinions are formed by their beliefs. By asking one of those simple questions, you will know if they are interested in CBD's health benefits or someone who wants to learn more about building their CBD MONEY TREE. Let the candidate see the opportunity –

Renita Brannan

not just you as an individual. Let the tools do the work for you. In fact, after you ask the above questions, send over "Intro to Kannaway" video from your app. It takes 30 seconds to text it! It is a fabulous TOOL! When you speak, speak with confidence about the company you represent. It's the end of the prohibition of cannabis! Forbes magazine projected 700% growth in the next two years! CNBC said CBD related annual revenue is projected to grow from $800 million to $22 Billion by 2022.

#8 Kannaway Share/Business Review

Learn how to effectively present Kannaway utilizing the tools (flipchart and a couple excellent short videos). This practice combines low-pressure business environment, casual and social atmospheres, and first-person testimonials. This is where Kannaway is unlike anything else we have ever done before. We realized very quickly we could build this business "virtually from home." I want to explain both ways of doing this; home or online. You choose which route is correct for you. I use a combination of both!

Kannaway events demonstrate how to launch a legal CBD business. Here's the format:

1. **Introduce yourself and briefly share WHY** you launched your Kannaway business.
2. **Ask all guests,** "What is your name and please tell me briefly why you are here."
3. **Opening Comments:** (Make this your own words or use something similar to ours.) We are at a pivotal point in our country and world history. It is the end of the prohibition of cannabis and massive wealth is about to be

created. People will experience an entirely new level of wellness. When people consume our incredible triple lab tested products, their bodies begin the restoration process. This is because you begin to nourish your endocannabinoid system. This important system in your body has been malnourished for nearly 80 years. CBD helps our bodies to regain that state of homeostasis and balance. Because of our high quality, efficacious products, we have an incredible financial opportunity at hand. People that are moving the cannabis message of physical and financial health by teaching others a system to do the same, are partaking in one of the biggest shifts we will see in this lifetime! In fact, more wealth will be created by this transition than any other in our country's history. It is bigger than the launch of the home computer. The trends of financial wealth associated with cannabis are a 700% increase in the next few years according to Forbes Magazine. Are you ready for the greenrush goldrush?

4. **Push play on "The Problem" video.** Available in back office or on app.

5. We don't focus solely on the problem, but we understand pain moves people. When looking at the "pain/pleasure principle," often times "pain" is a bigger motivator. Thankfully, we have a solution with Kannaway's products to nourish our endocannabinoid system. After showing the problem video, **push play on "Intro to Kannaway ".** We all want to be part of history changing and the company that continues to change history!

6. A well-nourished endocannabinoid system functions much better than a malnourished one. **Push play on**

"The Soil to Sale" video. This is a great video summarizing what makes our products so powerful in the marketplace. We are truly the world cannabis leader!

7. **Share a little personal commentary regarding the videos just watched.** As you are realizing, this is a "timing opportunity" but it is also "timeless." We are strategically positioned with the company of firsts to easily share this simple message of health/wealth creation through Kannaway's products and compensation plan with the world. The cannabis message will only continue to grow over the coming years. We are proud and fortunate to have partnered with the very best CBD company in the world! Kannaway has both the highest quality products as well as the best system to create unlimited financial freedom.

8. **Ask who's ready!** Are you ready to begin your health and wealth journey? For health-related questions, it is valuable to check out www.echoconnection.org. This resource has over 4000 medical studies on CBD/cannabis and various conditions. This is excellent resource to discover the science that exists with cannabis and the endocannabinoid system (ECS). Remember, make sure to say that Kannaway doesn't claim to treat, cure, or prevent disease (because only drug companies can say that - which is an entirely different book). We help the body to restore wellness by nourishing the endocannabinoid system to create homeostasis!

9. **Instruct guests how to get started.** If you are interested in building a business, get started with one of the Fast Start Value Packs. These provide an incredible savings and have a wide variety of products for you to

experience and love. By enrolling with the appropriate Fast Start kit, you can earn fast start bonuses if you sponsor 3 value packs in the first 30 days. As a FAST START QUALIFIED BRAND AMBASSADOR your first order bonuses, Kannaway calls it Direct Sales Commissions (DSC) will be TRIPLED on all value packs purchased in the first month for everyone you enroll for the life of your business.

$60 instead of $20
$225 instead of $75
$300 instead of $100
$450 instead of $150

10. **Over the next 10-15 minutes, we will review the 10 steps to success,** which is a New Member Orientation. It is the SYSTEM to follow if you are interested in creating six figures and beyond in Kannaway. Push play on the "GETTING STARTED" video found in the Kannaway Connect app or simply read through the "10 Steps to Success" in *back* office or on app. It has embedded links to help people to go deeper if necessary. Remember, you don't have to be wealthy to start. You do have to start to become wealthy. Even if you stumble through the 10 steps, the individuals with an abundance mindset will join your team and grow with you.

Establish dates for your Kannaway events.

Watch all Kannaway's videos in back office and app to prepare for your first event.

Event #1 Date _____

Event #2 Date _____

#9 New Member Orientation

Review the 10 steps to success. This can be done by watching the Getting Started video on your app and in your back office. In addition, the Getting Started Guide - 10 Steps to Success is in your back office as well as on your app. A few things to include in a New Member Orientation.

- Review Back Office and App – practice sending out links from app
- Set up Smartship of 110 PV or greater to maxout comp plan
- Review how to enroll new customers and BA's from app or website
- Become Fast Start Qualified for triple Direct Sales Commissions
- Set goals to go Fast Start 3000 (within 60 days) and Fast Start 9000 (within 90 days) - both are $1000 bonuses
- Review Payquicker - they will receive email and can set up account to receive commissions on Payquicker card or have money deposited into checking
- When to utilize Kannaway customer service or engage personal sponsor
- Importance of leveraging 3-way call so your sponsor can help you
- Enroller placement of new Brand Ambassadors (within 7 days of enrolling)
- Importance of www.echoconnection.org for research and to giving donations

#10 ACTION and DUPLICATION

The massive success formula is to consistently share with 3-5 new people per day. A fantastic goal is to enroll at least three customers and three Brand Ambassadors per month with a value pack.

"Knowing is not enough, we must apply. Willing is not enough, we must do."- Bruce Lee

CHAPTER 12

CATCH THE WAVE OR MISS THE WAVE

Reflecting on the vivid memories of the epic Hawaiian vacation Kannaway sent our family on, I reminisce about one special day. We had driven up the coastline from our resort to Poipu Bay. The sun and breeze were perfect to enjoy the pristine beach. Our boys grabbed their boards and paddled out towards some waves. We spent the afternoon bodyboarding, snorkeling, relaxing with inspiring books, and just breathing in the healing warmth and aroma of our surroundings. As the sun started to set, we met our boys on the beach with some freshly shaved ice flavored with organic pineapple and coconut. We gazed out at the sunset and breathtaking coastline. We listened to the majestic crashing waves echoing through the bay.

A handsome young elementary aged Hawaiian boy walked up and took in the moment with us. At 12 he was already very adept at all things surfing. Our boys asked

him a few questions and we listened as he
replied. "Catching a wave is one of the most exciting
things you can do in the world. There's really nothing else
like it," he said. He explained that nearly anyone and
everyone is capable. To catch a wave, you must
understand just a few things and learn to make decisions
quickly. First you must anticipate what's coming. Then
you must be in the correct position with your body and
your board. Next, it's all about paddling with both your
hands and arms. "Most people give up to soon." he said.
"They think they've done what it takes to ride the wave
and stop paddling. Then they miss out on what could've
been an epic ride!"

As we listened to his instructions, I couldn't help but
think of the parallels to surfing a big wave and changing
your life through the CBD MONEY TREE opportunity
we discuss in this book. The GREENRUSH is the
biggest wave we'll see in our lifetime! It's your chance to
be the BIG-KAHUNA! First you must have the vision
and instincts to anticipate what's coming. It helps to pay
attention to the projections. Remember CBD sales are
expected to surpass $22 Billion/year by 2022 and $57
billion by 2025. Next align yourself with the right
company and fastest growing team. Put yourself in a
position to win. Make the decision to go for it. Learn the
proven and predictable patterns of success and quickly
implement them. Focus on daily income producing
activities and go to work! Don't quit too early. Your
success is inevitable as you join the biggest health and
financial wave of the 21st Century.

Catching the perfect wave takes the following:

- Anticipate
- Capability
- Opportunity
- Action

Unlike most opportunities where a specific set of skills are required to succeed, a CBD MONEY TREE can be created by nearly anyone. Regardless of your ability to surf, your education, sales experience, business experience, or financial literacy, you can build a CBD MONEY TREE! We have successful members on our team ranging in age from 18-80. It's not about age or the amount of business or health experience. Creating wealth is about recognizing opportunities early. To do this, a person must have an open mind to something new. The wave is coming… and it's a BIG ONE! Is your mind open? Is your board positioned in the right direction to catch the wave? A close-minded person will base their decisions on what they already know and previously experienced. Of course, you already know what's in the past. Think about this for a minute. "People don't know what they don't know." If someone has suggested that you may be "close minded" simply ask yourself, "Have my decisions led to ultimate success and happiness? Has your past created the wealth and freedom you dream of?" Don't be too discouraged if you're not there yet. Your past prepares you for your future. Now is your time. Open your mind to opportunities, act with urgency and intent, develop new habits and change or accelerate the direction of your life!

When your capabilities come in alignment with a perfectly

timed opportunity, incredible success will occur. You will most likely never see a wave present itself to you like the end of the prohibition of cannabis and CBD again in your lifetime.

We love how Kannaway President, Blake Schroeder, mentioned his powerful paradigm shift towards this opportunity in his forward of this book. He simply looked around the room at his computers, clothing, phones, pictures, furniture, and the like. He asked himself if any of those industries would likely be larger 6 months or 6 years from now. Do you think the cannabis industry will be bigger 10 years from now? The big kahuna is coming! Can you anticipate your success?

The explosive financial growth in the CBD market is creating a new economy. This industry will produce more new revenue for those who participate than the introduction of the computer to our society! We've found network marketing magnifies the CBD opportunity.

As our mentor, Randy Schroeder, describes the opportunity, "Direct selling/network marketing is the single greatest training ground for an entrepreneur that exists. If one would throw his heart and soul into direct selling for the next five years, you will develop skills and character attributes not available anywhere else. It's the single biggest relationship building industry. The opportunity and relationship building that is developed in networking marketing is so broad that it completely transcends any other type of business."

Action is simple. It comes down to making a decision. Get up and move forward! We strongly believe building a

CBD MONEY TREE will create incredible success for anyone who acts with urgency and enthusiasm. Join our team and change your future! Success is inevitable! You only need the willingness to commit and act on the proven patterns of success.

Below are some recommended books to support you as you take the next step. Follow and message me on Facebook (Renita Rhone Brannan) and direct message me on Instagram at CBDMONEYTREE.

Further reading to support the growth of your CBD MONEY TREE and overall financial IQ:

The Richest Man in Babylon by George S. Clason

The Secrets of the Millionaire Mind by T. Harv Eker

Think and Grow Rich by Napoleon Hill

Becoming a Pioneer of Success by Tracey Armstrong

The Dream Giver by Bruce Wilkinson

The Seasons of Change by Jim Rohn

How to Win Friends and Influence People by Dale Carnegie

The Bible - Excellent leadership wisdom and lessons of love, courage, faith, forgiveness, grace

REAL LIFE STORIES – CBD MONEY TREE PIONEERS

The following accounts are personal stories from our friends and team members. While honoring their stories, we must remind you that Kannaway CBD does not treat, mitigate, or cure disease. It simply helps the body to restore homeostasis.

We invite you to enjoy the following stories from our team members who made the decision to join Kannaway and build their very own CBD MONEY TREE.

These are Real Life Success Stories…. Some are just getting started and many have had tremendous financial success already! Keep in mind, individual results may vary depending on your willingness to implement the proven system.

Beau Brannan – North Dakota

I started my Kannaway business at 18 years old, just a senior in high school. A health scare initiated my family and me to research CBD. Thankfully, I was cleared of any health concerns but during that time I learned enough about CBD to understand it would help me in several areas of health. I've consumed Kannaway Pure CBD now for almost 2 years. Among other things, it helps me handle stress and anxiety.

Most of you probably know this but it's not always easy as a teenager. We have pressure, stress and anxiety. I did a research paper my freshman year of college on teenage anxiety and depression. We're growing up in this fast-paced world where it's normal for middle and high school kids to have a daily grande mocha latte with a double shot of expresso and extra whip cream! Rockstars and redbulls are in every locker room and high school parking lot! Of high school students that drink nearly 60% of them are binge drinkers and college statistics even worse. Sugar, caffeine, alcohol all increase anxiety and depression! It's no wonder anxiety is the most common mental illness in the U.S. affecting over 40 million adults! Anxiety and depression are very treatable but less than 40% of people with anxiety seek help! Is it safe to use prescribed meds for anxiety and depression anyway? Have you seen the list of side effects in common anxiety and depression prescribed medications? Why would you give your teenager a prescribed drug with a side effect of hallucination or possible suicide?! It's really time to wake up in this country!! Do the research and make better decisions. Protect yourself and your family!!

Other areas of personal health where CBD has helped me is sleeping better and recovering from workouts. As a NCAA track athlete, I can't consume CBD with even a trace of THC. I'm thankful Kannaway has third party testing and certificates of analysis that shows exactly what's in each bottle. I know and trust I'm getting only pure CBD. It's legal, safe, and effective.

While health has been the focus of my testimony up until now it's really the business and financial opportunity that keeps me fired up. I've qualified for Kannaway's minimum income guarantee every month and have earned over $60,000 in less than 2 years. We recently experienced an all-inclusive trip to Costa Rica. Let me tell you, Kannaway really knows how to throw a party!!! Owning a business I can work from my phone, sending out short clips, and links that educate and inspire people to consider these products is so helpful and easy. I use the Kannaway Connect app every day. I don't have to pretend to be the Dr. or health expert. I share links, get notified when my contact views videos, and follow up when I'm prompted with an alert on my phone! I'm confident we have the very best CBD in the world and that helps me when contacting others.

Listen, I get the MLM stigma and opinion of some people regarding network marketing is not always positive. But from my perspective, it's truly the business of the 21s century! It may have been weird to shop for products online or direct from companies 20 years ago. But I'm just 19! Not only is it no longer weird... shopping online or from our phones is the preferred method to consume products for my peers and me! We communicate with everyone through social media apps, shop, book travel, get directions, find restaurants, bank, invest, and pay bills on our phone or online. We want our voice to be heard so referrals and rating products is just part of everyday life!

I couldn't be more excited for the future of this company. I'm so thankful to the incredible leaders that support my business growth! My CBD MONEY TREE is planted and thriving!

I encourage anyone reading this book to find me and reach out:

insta @ beaubrannan
snap @ bbrannan_m
tiktok @ beaubrannan

I'm ready to run with any young entrepreneur that wants to go after success! Sky is the limit!!

Ashley Brossart – North Dakota

Kannaway CBD products continue to have a significant positive impact on my family's health and overall wellbeing!

In October of 2018, my father was diagnosed with stage 4 prostate cancer with metastasis to the bones. While waiting for his oral chemo medication to be approved my father started taking various Kannaway CBD products. In just 3 short weeks, his PSA lab value went from >1400 down to 31.7. Four months of Kannaway CBD and oral chemo treatment and my father was in remission. Bone scan in March was cancer free!

My mother had an unsuccessful neck operation but has been able to discontinue pain killers and muscle relaxers after consuming Kannaway CBD.

My husband who's suffered from debilitating migraines for years has finally found relief since starting Kannaway CBD.

Our 22-month-old son gets GI relief when given Kannaway CBD oil. It also alleviates his teething pain.

As for myself, I noticed a huge difference in mental clarity, energy and mood. I'm able to deal with stress much better. I sleep soundly, which is something I've never been able to do. I consumed Kannaway Pure Gold CBD oil throughout my second pregnancy and found that it helped alleviate nausea, swelling, and pain. After my c-section, my Dr. was impressed that I had less than normal blood loss. My son was born a healthy 9lb 8oz with zero health problems.

An added bonus to the health benefits is the wealth benefit of Kannaway. I quickly paid back my original start-up cost and earned more than enough to cash flow the low monthly expenses. In just three short months I was able to rank advance to area director and earn a minimum income guarantee of $2,500/month! I simply share my personal experiences and the products with others. Kannaway has truly blessed my life. As a registered nurse, I truly believe we could change the world if more providers would integrate Kannaway CBD into their practices.

Alana Reynolds - California

I am a passionate soul, obsessed with living life to the fullest, as our happiest most authentic selves. I am a wife and a mother to three gifts from God, an 18-year-old beautiful daughter and two bubbly baby boys. I am also an autoimmune warrior, a grateful recovering addict and a victim turned victor. Family, faith, freedom and love is the foundation for everything in my life. Love above all.

When my health took a turn again, I refused to become a victim to my circumstances once more. I refused to go back to a time when my husband couldn't give me a hug or even an affectionate hand on the shoulder because I was so tender. The discomfort throughout my body was so out of control. I refused to go back to being exhausted all the time, beyond moody and just down in the dumps. I refused to allow doctors to just throw medications at me without knowing what was going on and without being able to tell me that they would help – because they didn't. I decided I wouldn't go back, but I didn't know how to move forward either. What was my next step? I had no clue.

I've seen benefits from optimal nutrition, exercise, meditation, yoga, acupuncture, and float therapy. You name it. I've tried it or I'm still doing it. All these things have been helpful, even allowing us to grow our family. But after our last son, I found myself exhausted by mid-day. I had a sore throat; mild fever and my hands were barely functional. My hands hurt so badly I could barely hold the steering wheel or open a bottle for our baby. The business I had built for nearly 5 years was also in danger of being abandoned, which would be a huge financial blow to our family.

I went to work researching what else was out there that might be able to help me jump back in the game of life as my 100% happiest self. When I have brain fog and pain, when I can't play with my kids or be truly present for a conversation with my husband or daughter, I am NOT my happiest self. We all deserve to be happy!

In my weeks and weeks of research, I kept circling back to CBD oil. I discovered how hemp was different than marijuana and how our Endocannabinoid System helps regulate pain sensations, moods, appetite, memory and other cognitive processes, even our immune system. I was astonished yet highly skeptical. I was desperate. If it's helping all these people I'm reading about, why wouldn't it help me too? Maybe it won't work for me, but I'll never know unless I give it a serious shot.

While I had tried some CBD oil in the past, I didn't find it beneficial. I also didn't know that not all CBD oil was created equal. This time around, I wasn't about to bank my health and the well-being of my family's future on anything subpar. Once again, I got to work researching the mountains of CBD products and companies out there. Time and time again I kept coming back to Kannaway.

Legality. Quality. Reliability. Integrity. Heart.

Kannaway had the qualities that mattered to me and they seemed to have the products that I could count on consistently. At the time, they were the only fully federally legal supplier of CBD in the US and in 40 countries worldwide. They were the first publicly traded cannabis company in the world and the leaders in this industry. If they were good enough to be asked to speak at the World Health Organization hearings on CBD, maybe they would be good enough for me too.

I learned Kannaway offered a Brand Ambassador program. I knew if these products worked for me, I'd want to share them with family and friends. Why not get these products for free, create even more financial freedom for our family and help make a massive impact in others' lives along the way?! I looked closely at the Kannaway compensation plan. With a background in finance and network marketing, I knew this was an opportunity I couldn't pass up. I spoke with my mentors, prayed on it and pulled the trigger!

Well, within a week of consuming Kannaway CBD, my health substantially improved. Thank God! Not once have I been bogged down nor unable to use my hands and I awake feeling more refreshed and excited for life than ever! With CBD having such a wide range of benefits, I quickly found that sharing this gift was fairly simple. Family and friends soon joined me and with just a couple of social media posts, I realized how much interest was already out there regarding CBD oil. I also noticed how much misinformation was out there as well.

With every bit of information I'd share, I was amazed at the astounding response! Within one month of putting these products into my body, I was earning enough in just ONE WEEK to more than cover a car payment! I continue to be amazed at this opportunity as the interest is growing by leaps and bounds. Plus, the messages of the benefits people are experiencing are pouring in.

The time to make a massive impact on our world's health and wealth is now and it's with Kannaway! The health benefits of CBD oil are undeniable and over 50,000 products can be made from hemp, which has a negative carbon footprint on our environment. The end of the prohibition of cannabis in the US is about to blast this industry and our businesses into even more massive momentum. It was pretty scary jumping into a new business, but I am so glad I did a swan dive in!

Pam Kostelecky – North Dakota

I've lived in North Dakota most of my life, with a few years spent in Florida and Colorado. Without giving away my age, which you may want to know... I am eligible for social security, married, with children and grandchildren all living within my community. Throughout my adult life God has been my true north, my husband has never set limits on what I could do and always believed I could do anything. What a lucky charm he is to me.

Though I was an honor student all through high school, I never went to college. I've had numerous jobs to earn a side hustle without too much commitment. I've enjoyed a 13-year career in business banking and have taught almost every type of fitness class invented since 1982. Jane Fonda, leg warmers, "I'm a Maniac" ring a bell with anyone? I'm the free spirit who wanted to travel and experience the world. I wanted a family. I wanted to teach exercise. Those things have not changed.

My WHY for CBD is critical. Our family is riddled with Alzheimer's. My sister was officially diagnosed at age 52 and passed at 63. We feel she was 47 when we first started seeing signs of confusion. My mother has been diagnosed with dementia, her sister is in the Alzheimer's unit, her brother passed with Alzheimer's. For years I have had my pulse on my own symptom of the disease, always testing myself for signs.

About a year ago my daughter started sending me information on CBD for Alzheimer's. I thought it was marijuana so I didn't read the articles. During that time, I felt I was possibly experiencing the same symptoms I saw with my sister's early stages of the disease. Normally I'm very outgoing but I began to withdraw from conversations because I was having difficulty finding words. I have always been confident in myself but that was beginning to change, and I was afraid.

I finally did it, I scheduled a memory test. The testing took me about three and half hours, was difficult and extremely irritating. It was just prior to testing that my daughter asked if I'd read the articles on CBD for Alzheimer's. I told her I hadn't and to her surprise I said I had scheduled a memory test. It was at that point I was ready to look at CBD.

We met with Renita Brannan about CBD and Kannaway. I poured myself into researching CBD for legality and scientific data on the health benefits. What I found was truly mind blowing. After a week I simply asked myself, "Five years from now do you want to say "I'm so glad I did" or "I wish I had?" I can tell you now- that I'm glad I did and I didn't have to wait five years to say it.

Within 3 days on CBD I noticed a difference in mental clarity and sharpness. Though I've always had good energy within a month I noticed I had even better energy that lasted all day. I normally have a good vibe but after two months I felt I was responding more gently and didn't react sharply to things that may have triggered my cynical side, particularly with the husband. My confidence is back, and my zeal for a long, healthy, happy life is thriving.

My mother was one of my first customers. Prior to CBD she lived in a state of depression. For two years she would not enter into conversation with me, wouldn't leave her room, often crying and confused. She is now conversing. Her caregivers have commented that she is more social and happier. She has occasional bouts of depression because of her diagnosis but is able to get out of them without medication. She sleeps well and has a good appetite. I am so very grateful to have gotten her on CBD and back into reality and living. With CBD my goal is to keep her independently living in her apartment until she leaves this earth.

I never intended to work the business side of CBD but how could I not? The money was real and Fast Start Qualification could help me pay for our family's products. I found myself again asking the same question, "Five years from now will I find myself saying I'm glad I did or I wish I had?" Once again, I can tell you I'm glad I did and I didn't have to wait five years to say it.

I put my ego aside and quickly jumped in. Reaching that first goal of Fast Start set the momentum in motion. Social media made it easy to share the CBD message. Traditional media of television, newspapers, and magazines was heralding our message. Washington was fighting our battle. The cat was out of the box and it wasn't going back in.

Kannaway was the only choice for me. I wanted a company that aligned with my standards. A company with integrity that I could trust that would consistently deliver high quality CBD. A company with strong leadership that was financially equipped for growth. Kannaway was that company. From its origin they have set the Gold Standard as a company of firsts. Innovative technologies with new products being released for every mammal that has an endocannabinoid system. Kannaway has products that are either singularly unique with no other product like it on the market or milligram per milligram Kannaway products are competitively priced with similarly marketed CBD products.

The financial opportunity in the cannabis market is a no brainer. The financial opportunity in direct selling is unlimited. Put the two together, with the right company, and that formula is magical. Kannaway is that company. Again, a company of firsts, first in the direct selling industry to distribute federally legal CBD in the US. World-renowned leaders in the direct selling industry teaching and training so we can maximize the compensation plan at every level.

At a time in life when I could be looking at slowing down, I am enthusiastically participating in something great. It is the end of the prohibition of cannabis! Restored health, longevity, professional and personal growth are a daily blessing. Without limits, this free spirit is soaring into her golden years with liquid Pure Gold and Kannaway.

Jessica Brossart – North Dakota

I have been an entrepreneur my whole life, including 13 years as an alternative health practitioner with a practice in Rugby, ND. Although I absolutely loved my work & clients, when my business partner moved on, I decided to seek a new challenge. I wanted to help local entrepreneurs and I was quickly hired to be the Executive Director of our local Job Development Authority. It was the first "9 to 5" job I've ever had and I soon realized that a government job moved much too slow for me. it was not the positive work environment I was used to, so I started looking for a new opportunity.

I had heard that CBD made from hemp was becoming legal and saw it as the opportunity to reopen my practice.

I researched many different companies and narrowed it down to a few serious contenders. I then examined each thoroughly to decide what CBD product I would feel confident sharing with my clients.

Kannaway stood out beyond all other CBD companies in their quality, safety, and higher potency products. I tried one of their CBD oils and after 2 days I found that I felt happier, more peaceful and content... even at that stressful job! It was at that moment that I wanted to share more happiness with the world!

We also tried CBD for our dog. He was a large breed farm dog who had been hit by a car a couple years prior which left with him with only 3 legs. He was having a harder time with his mobility. We had given him hemp (no CBD) treats earlier which helped a bit. But now he would lay on his rug in our farm shop & whimper in pain. We gave him a couple of the Kannaway CBD treats a day and he snapped out of it within a day or two!

I joined Kannaway as a brand ambassador to start sharing CBD oil with my clients. After more success with the products, I decided to start my health practice again by adding their CBD products. Using the B2B option, I can get Kannaway products at an even bigger discount.

During my time at the JDA, I realized that our town needs more consumer opportunity for its residents. Several gift shops had closed. I began looking for a larger space to open and began creating a whole new store front with more to offer our community.

My new store, Market on Main, is a 2500 square foot space. We have over 30 consigners of unique handmade gifts & homemade goodies… & of course, the highest quality & potency CBD products! I have also been blessed to employ my good friend who is also on my Kannaway team & a high school intern through our school's co-op program.

I truly feel that I could not have achieved opening my new store without Kannaway and the guidance of Renita and Scott. Not only was I able to completely replace my income from the beginning of opening Market on Main, I am also helping my community and entrepreneurs in a more impactful way!

Shari McCants- Kansas

What's your life purpose? I found mine. I'm a wife, mother, and own my own lucrative CBD business. My husband, Matt, is an engineer and very supportive of my new-found passion! We also have two beautiful teenagers, Reid, 17, and Taylor, 16.

Close to Home

In 2010, doctors diagnosed Reid with Type 1 Diabetes, and my family's world turned upside down. After pricking his poor fingers 8-10 times a day to check his blood sugars, he administers insulin based on his carb intake. Type 1 diabetes is an autoimmune disease and despite active research, has no cure. Treatment focuses on managing blood sugar levels with insulin, diet, and lifestyle to prevent complications, which are numerous. Doctors say that when a diabetic's blood sugar is regular, they are in homeostasis, which means they can maintain internal stability.

What Nutrition School Missed

I became a licensed nutritionist to help Reid, but my training didn't include what is probably the essential fact that every person should know. Five years into teaching and coaching nutrition, I discovered that our bodies have a single system (Endocannabinoid system) that regulates mood, sleep, appetite, balance, and metabolism called the endocannabinoid system. When the system is healthy, we are in homeostasis. That's what Reid didn't have!

With more research, I came across something called CBD oil, which is naturally occurring in hemp plants. Before 1937, hemp grew abundantly in the United States. The farmers cultivated it for over 50,000 different commercial products, including domestic animal feed. Every time we ate steak, chicken, bacon, eggs, etc. we got CBD oil. That is because the animals were feeding on it. It was part of our food chain. People living in the US consumed an average of around 50 milligrams a day.

Outlawing Cannabis

But, for political and economic reasons some powerful individuals in the US managed to get the Marijuana Tax Act of 1937 passed. This new law outlawed the entire cannabis plant, and taxed hemp so heavily no one could afford to grow it. The story is fascinating. Today's popular opinion was influenced without real knowledge of why and how cannabis and thus hemp and its derivatives became illegal.

What Science and the Medical Profession Know Today

It's taken scientists and medical professionals over 75 years to discover the correlation between the elimination of CBD oil in our diets and the numerous modern diseases that plague us today, like Diabetes, Parkinson's, Alzheimer's, Autism, ADHD, Fibromyalgia, Eczema, Psoriasis, Chronic Fatigue, Irritable Bowel Syndrome, Cancer, and dozens more. Our bodies are CBD deficient and therefore unable to maintain homeostasis. A new clinical term has emerged: Clinical Endocannabinoid Deficiency Syndrome.

My Obsession

If CBD could help bring homeostasis for Reid and his Type 1 Diabetes, I was all in. I became obsessed and researched via the Echoconnection website (www.echoconnection.org). This online library of cannabis related clinical studies and articles showed the possibility of helping millions of people suffering from hundreds of conditions, not just diabetics.

Searching for the most trusted source of CBD for my family, I discovered Kannaway to be the very best. Kannaway is a company of firsts and a real pioneer in the cannabis industry. One of the recent accomplishments is that the founder, Dr Titus was chosen to address the FDA about CBD.

The Journey

I started my journey with Kannaway on January 4, 2018. It has been a rush – a green rush – for me. Once I got started, the floodgates opened. I feel God has a plan for my life and I'm taking my nutritional business to the next level. My initial desire was to help others, but I have discovered the financial benefits to be unparalleled.

I have a God-given talent and love talking to people, and I see sharing the benefits of CBD a blessing. I find myself chatting with someone and the next thing I know several others have joined the conversation to get information and knowledge. It's not a sales job for me.

I reached out to family, friends, and former nutrition clients and followed the fantastic 10-steps to Success "Fast-Start program", which required I sponsor three people purchasing a value pack either as a Customer or as a Brand Ambassador. I did it in one week! Now I get triple bonuses for the life of my business. My next goals were Fast Start 3000 and 9000, which were both $1000 bonuses. I accomplished both easily and received a $1000 bonus each for the achievements. In 2 years, I've sponsored 80 people, 20 customers, and multiple storefronts. The storefronts are great. It's fun to enroll established businesses and help them find new ways to increase their revenue and ultimately take care of their current customers/clients with the highest quality products in the marketplace.

Today, I enjoy one-on-ones with interested networkers, share on social media (Facebook, Instagram, and LinkedIn) and realize it's all about education. So many people are still confused about the difference between Hemp and Marijuana.

Invest in Yourself and Your Family

Yes, there is an initial investment as there is with any business, but I love how Kannaway positions you to win. The Echoconnection website is an excellent resource for knowledge and support with thousands of peer-reviewed clinical studies from medical and scientific communities. The ease of access to professional videos from our Kannaway Connect app help the products and business sell themselves. You don't sell; you educate. You share a message that is changing the world.

I am so excited about the future. I love that I am helping change history and that I get to help so many people, especially my son. The financial opportunity has been incredible for my family, but my dream is to one day have a world without Type 1 diabetes.

It's simple, Kannaway is the innovator, not the imitator. Let's all get healthy, not high!

Kannaway Firsts:

- Kannaway's parent company is Medical Marijuana Inc, the first publicly traded cannabis company in the US. Ticker symbol MJNA. You can earn up to 4 million shares through the compensation program, which is just one of the many perks.
- First direct sales marketing company to offer cannabis products.
- First to establish a global CBD pipeline, making cannabidiol and other beneficial cannabinoids available all over the world.
- First to deliver cannabis brands across the US

state lines and international borders, making the products available in all 50 US states and dozens of countries.

- First to develop strict quality standards for cannabis products, including rigorous triple lab testing.
- First to introduce CBD foods and supplements to the mainstream marketplace.
- First to create a mainstream, natural, botanical CBD brand.
- First with a license to commercialize the US National Institutes of Health patent "Cannabinoids as Antioxidants and Neuroprotectants." Patent #6630507
- First to introduce legal medical cannabis products to Brazil, Mexico, Puerto Rico, and Paraguay.
- First to deliver prescription CBD products through Hemp Meds for Epilepsy, Alzheimer's, Parkinson's, chronic pain and migraine sufferers.
- First to offer government-subsidized, botanical, cannabis-based products.
- First company to have cannabis products subsidized by the Brazilian government.

I'm proud of my choice for other reasons too.

- Our corporate leaders and sister companies playing a role in changing federal laws in multiple countries and were asked to speak regarding CBD before the World Health Organization.
- Our products have been on the Doctors TV show, Dateline, NBC, CBS, and the History Channel along with several other major media

sources.

- Kannaway created a nonprofit, www.echoconnection.org for people who depend on CBD but can't afford it. They have given over 1.3 million dollars of CBD away to families in need.

- Kannalife Sciences is first and only company to hold licensing rights to patent 6630507 to create CBD product treatment and prevention of strokes and concussions. The only company with National Football League alumni partners who dedicate themselves to sharing the message in hopes of preventing and treating Chronic Traumatic Encephalopathy (CTE).

Blake and Heather Reis - North Dakota

My name is Heather Reis and my husband's name is Blake. We have four amazing, fun, loving, crazy, children. Blake is a Journeyman Lineman and works for a local electric company. I currently run my own in-home daycare, along with teaching SkyFit (a fitness class) at SkyZone. Blake and I also aid in helping others as Brand Ambassadors to start their own journeys with Kannaway. I also like to help with our children's program at church whenever I can. With our spare time Blake and I like to spend time with family, vacation as much as possible, exercise, work on home projects, crafts, bake, volleyball, and hockey.

I first met Renita Brannan attending classes at SkyZone. She introduced me to this miraculous product we know as CBD. Blake and I were fortunate to not have had any prior health issues or concerns before taking CBD but were intrigued on the many health benefits this product had to offer. Everything I read about CBD, I kept thinking, why wouldn't we take this product? Why isn't everyone taking this product? Every article I read amazed me, and continues to, with life changing testimonies all the way to overturning and changing laws in other countries. After researching more about the product and what it could do for our health and wealth, we signed up right away. We immediately shared with family and friends. Blake and I were completely hooked from the start. It only took us a couple days to start seeing results. Our entire family was sleeping better without playing musical beds at night.

Blake and I both noticed we were more focused, rested, and energized. We no longer fought with our 6-year-old to get up and get ready for school. We don't have to battle with him in the morning countless times to sit down and eat his meal or after school when completing his homework. The overall feeling of wellness this product provides to our family is more than enough reason to be lifelong consumers.

Blake and I researched other products and quickly realized that Kannaway was the highest quality product in the market place. The science that backs up the purity and triple lab testing is hands down the best of the best of all other brands of CBD. Kannaway is a company of many firsts and continues to remain on top. This company has played a huge role in changing laws in various countries. Our CBD is also prescribed in three countries for numerous ailments. I have witnessed several doctors express their views on taking CBD and have only perceived positive feedback. There is no other product that I have ever taken that did not include a possible side effect of some kind. CBD helps to restore homeostasis, which can help everyone's body.

As we started sharing Kannaway's products and our own family's testimonies with our friends and family we soon realized that it was easy to make money with this company. I have been a part of a lot of direct sales companies and Kannaway's compensation plan is leaps and bounds better than any of them. The money I would make with previous companies would have to go into inventory that I literally still have in my basement stored away. We can now use this income on the side for finishing projects around the house, paying off existing debt, and most importantly making the best memories traveling with my family. We love Kannaway!

Jennifer Long - Massachusetts

My name is Jennifer Long. I am a mother to three incredible boys, Kadin (15), Micah (8) and Levi (19 months), a registered nurse, nutritionist, holistic health and wellness enthusiast and professional. I am someone who takes pride in the knowledge I've worked hard to acquire as well as the desire to learn what I have yet to.

I am someone who has a passion to educate the public with accurate, up to date and relevant health and wellness research and developments. More importantly, I am always looking to improve the health and financial stability of my family. After seven years and seven different medications to "treat" my oldest child's ADHD symptoms, I had simply had it with pharmaceuticals. Every attempted medication was one stressful failed attempt after another and all that was left behind was side effects and tears. In my desperate attempt to help my son, I went to work to research "natural alternatives for ADHD." This search led me over and over to the same thing, CBD. As a nurse I had not even heard of this, but my interest was piqued. After researching thoroughly, I decided THIS WAS IT! Ok, so now that I knew CBD was the plan, I had to decide on a company to order it from. Being that I put such a strong effort into nutrition/health and this was going into my child's body, I wanted THE VERY BEST! That search led me to Kannaway.

Kannaway had credibility that impressed me both morally and scientifically, as a mother and nurse. Every line I read I was nodding, smiling and getting more excited. Every video I watched, my heart was racing and things just started to click. Then the "Aha" moment! I could actually make this a business? I could improve my child and my entire family's health AND provide sustainable income as well? This was a no brainer and I immediately got to work sharing the health and opportunity of a LEGAL CANNABIS BUSINESS in January 2018. The first night I shared my new Kannaway adventure on Facebook, my phone was going off nonstop. Message after message, comment after comment and even texts and phone calls were pouring in. I could barely keep the charge as I answered people until 2-3am.

What I didn't realize was that this opportunity was coming at the most crucial time. I was at that time seven months pregnant and had no idea that my maternity leave was about to begin earlier than planned. As a home care nurse, my position had to be filled, what I expected to be temporarily turned into permanently. When I was ready to return to work, I was informed that my position was no longer available. Wait, I was replaced? Your job is not guaranteed people, and I learned this the hard way.

Fortunately for me, my amazing longtime friend and previous business partner, Renita had called me in January and we began to build this CBD MONEY TREE. It was because of that call to action, and my drive to act, I was able to REPLACE my nursing income quickly. I have paid my mortgage, cell phone bills, have bought groceries, pampered myself with manicures and dinners out. The best thing is that I have never once paid for my CBD products and we use about $300-400 worth a month. Guaranteed income is a security everyone needs, wants and deserves. Not only am I making this happen for myself, I am helping my team succeed with their businesses and health as well. It makes me happy seeing the success of others and getting the phone calls and texts saying, "Jen, I made this much?" never gets old. It shows me that everyone can build this. You don't have to be a health professional, or even know how to talk about CBD. You just need to have a willingness to open your mouth and share. The duplicatable tools make it easy. The business is so simple and everything is accessible with a push of a button. Kadin has had a tremendous decrease in ADHD symptoms, everyone is healthier, and my CBD business is flourishing.

Rob and Mandy Hummel - Nevada

My wife Mandy and I are a young couple raising four kids that are very active in many extra-curricular activities out in Sparks, Nevada. Mandy is a full-time hairdresser, mother, wife and workout fanatic that loves spending time with our family. I am a full-time high school Physical Education/Weight Training teacher, Kannaway business owner, varsity football and track/field coach, youth football/basketball coach, father, and husband that also loves to spend time with my family. Needless to say, we keep ourselves busy. There are only two rare occurrences in the Hummel house, an open weekend and dull moments.

Mandy and I are both very passionate about health and fitness. We want to teach our children how to live healthy lifestyles and there is no better way than to model healthy behaviors for them to witness day in and day out. Our desire to live long healthy lives is what led us to look at CBD and Kannaway. Before January of 2018, we had no idea what the endocannabinoid system was or how taking CBD could benefit our health and overall well-being. We received a call one evening from our good friend Renita Brannan and she was so excited to tell us about Kannaway, that I knew it had to be something great!

Renita sent me a few links to check out the company and learn more about CBD and the endocannabinoid system. I then spent the next week researching as much information as I could find. Through the time that I spent researching, I became fascinated with all of the new information. At the same time, I was frustrated that I had never heard about the body's largest self-regulatory system (Endocannabinoid System), after having been a health/physical education major in college. After my own experience, I realized that the majority of people worldwide were also probably uninformed about this information, which caused me to think about things from a business perspective. I decided that a real financial opportunity in this market is going to exist at this special timing in history and I needed to find the right company.

I quickly found out that things in the CBD marketplace are very controversial in some states and that since CBD products are not regulated, quality and purity are a huge factor. Considering my profession and influence as an educator, I wanted to make sure that I was part of a company that was doing things 100% legally. I also wanted to be part of a company that was offering the best possible products and compensation mechanism for its' business builders. After looking at what was available, I quickly realized that no company compared to the one that Renita introduced me to initially.

Kannaway's products were the first in the industry and are second to absolutely none in terms of their quality, purity, and quantity. Their third-party triple lab testing standards are unlike any other company in this space because they truly care about their customers. The company's leadership structure, product developers, and scientific researchers are world renown and are creating the most cutting-edge products available. Finally, the company's charitable foundation and overall community display the genuine goodness that this company represents and made us WANT to become part of what Kannaway is all about. Therefore, my wife and I decided to become Kannaway business builders and haven't looked back.

The products have benefited us tremendously even though we are fortunate enough not to have any serious health conditions and would be considered by medical professionals as a healthy family. Our entire household, including our dog are consuming Kannaway's CBD products. We have all noticed a tremendous improvement in our sleep, energy levels, and focus. My son's skin condition has gone away, my pain from old sports injuries has been significantly reduced, and we had the peace of mind knowing that our three boys had neuro protectors around their brain via CBD throughout the football season and will for years to come.

We are currently working to build a team of like-minded people and our journey is about to gain a lot of momentum. We have made a significant amount of money and earned thousands of dollars of free products thus far, but it's only the beginning. Our initial goal was to make extra money, but the potential of this business has caused us to shift our mindset. We now plan to eventually replace the income of our current professions and obtain financial freedom. We once believed that time freedom and the lifestyle we've been seeking were not realistic goals, but Renita's leadership and Kannaway have changed that for us. We now know that our financial future with this company is limitless when we make a commitment to successful business building activities. Timing in business is everything and opportunities like this don't come around very often. Kannaway is the right company with the right products, leadership, and compensation at most importantly, the right time. We are about to go on an adventure and it's going to be one hell of a ride!

Josh and Brekka Lengenfelder - North Dakota

We are Joshua and Brekka Lengenfelder. We are a busy family of six and live by the motto "work hard and play even harder." We have been married for five years and have a 5-year-old boy, Toby, twin daughters, Hazel and Adeline, who are 4 and were born on Toby's 1st birthday! Yeah that's right, they all three have the same birthday! We also have a fun loving, adorable 19th month old Zanna.

We own a landscaping/ snow removal business in Bismarck/ Mandan that keeps Josh busy. Brekka works for the US Department of Labor as a Wage and Hour Investigator and has been a member of the North Dakota National Guard for 18 years! We recently purchased some land from Josh's aunt and uncle and live on 20 acres outside of Bismarck where we have built our forever home and plan to grow old.

In our free time our family likes to spend time outdoors. We enjoy camping, fishing, hunting, exercising, going to grandma and grandpa's house, riding our bikes, and just getting dirty! In the winter we love ice fishing, snowmobiling, and building fires in our fireplace.

When we discovered Kannaway CBD, we decided to jump in with both feet. The fact that the company triple lab tests all of their products for purity and quality was a big factor for us. We are also looking for a more natural approach with our overall health and Kannaway is second to none. In a short amount of time we have experienced great health benefits, and also have been loving the additional income by just sharing information with our friends and family. Some of the health benefits we have noticed are amazing sleep! This has been a game changer for us, we have a daughter who was having some problems falling asleep and staying asleep and after a few days on the products she is falling asleep shortly after going to bed, and is sleeping through the night. We love waking up feeling rested and are actually dreaming while sleeping, which hadn't been the case before CBD. We have also noticed our overall digestive system is working a lot better. Overall, we feel our health is better.

We live a very busy life and are excited to be feeling great! Earning an income while doing so has been a blast! We both have great paying jobs however there are always bills to be paid, diapers to be purchased, and daycare and preschool expenses. Having the extra income that we have earned through Kannaway has been a huge blessing to our family.

Kyle and Jacinta Engelhardt- North Dakota/Arizona

I was getting ready to board a plane in December of 2017 for a much-anticipated two-week vacation to Mexico. I got an intense call from my friend, Renita, saying, "Jacinta, this CBD thing is going to be BIG! Get a post on Facebook that you're involved." I thought, "Are you kidding, NOW? Do you know I am getting on an airplane in less than an hour? My knowledge of CBD is pretty much next to NOTHING!?" We had very brief snippets of discussions over the last year about CBD. Neither of us had EVER smoked pot. What would people think about us entering into the cannabis industry? What was the difference between marijuana and hemp? Very quickly I learned that CBD derived from hemp was NON-PSYCHOACTIVE. It basically helped get you healthy not high. Would CBD be a good business decision for us operating in our ultra conservative home state of ND? I just knew from Renita's tone of urgency this was a JUST DO, don't ask questions… JUST TRUST ME call. I made the post with her help, boarded my plane and when I arrived at our room in Mexico a few hours later I opened my texts and messages. IT WAS UNBELIEVABLE! How did ALL these people messaging me (young to many years older than me) even KNOW about CBD and the colossal health benefits that came with it? So as not to disturb my family members, I sat in the bathroom until 3:30 am answering messages all the while doing searches for answers to people's questions. As phone service was sketchy, I texted her immediately upon seeing all the messages, "Here is my credit card info, order us the largest kit with all the products so we can know the product, we want to be part of this business, Kyle and I are all in!!!!"

We both grew up and were raised in a small town in ND. Both of our parents were business owners and self-employed. I was the only girl invited to Kyle's 1st grade birthday party. We married one year out of high school. Kyle put his Business Degree to use by working as a nursing home administrator for ten years after he graduated from college. I held hourly paying jobs and also worked many years for my parents at their business while raising our children. We now own and operate J & K Grain Bin Sales & Construction for 30 plus successful years. We have been married for 40 years and have five adult children; Jeremy, Kyle, Alexander, Jordan and Katrina, and seven grandchildren. We earned an above average income that came with a cost to Kyle's health and at times division and strife within our family. Our grain bin business requires physically hard long hours. All of our children and most of our grandchildren have been employed at one time or another with us. We were both blessed to have come from homes where Christian principles were taught and we were raised on a Christian foundation. We just knew divorce would never be an option for us and that we would work diligently to obtain a lifestyle we wanted. And when we came up short financially, we just went out and worked some more. We were taught there were no free handouts.

Fast forward to 12 years ago, I signed on with our first network marketing company. We were passionate about the product, consumed the product and believed in it. We did have some financial success but nothing that was lifelong altering, and we only had a few on our team that were making residual income. We did learn the valuable business lesson of the importance of residual income. Residual income is money that is earned on a recurring basis. Rather than earning an hourly wage or a one-time commission on each of our sales like in our traditional business, residual income is generated through an initial monthly compensation from a monthly commitment of product. That concept is still proving itself true today with the $200 monthly payment we are still being paid each month from our efforts invested in our first Network Marketing company even though we have not worked that business for years. It's like a Christmas present each month. The more residual income you can build, the closer it will put you to your financial goals. I have read that the average millionaire has 7 different streams of income. One of the things that attracts us to network marketing is the vast possibilities of helping others not only with their heath but providing a level playing field for anyone who has a desire to have financial wealth. Through residual income, one can fulfill their dreams that many have forgotten about. We have been taught since we were young not to talk about 3 things in public: Religion, money and politics. It is just recently that I have been verbalizing those are the most important three things to talk about! How else do we learn if we don't talk and listen to experiences in these areas that are so relevant to our success?

This Kannaway CBD opportunity comes at the end of the prohibition of cannabis. People have realized that these products can be beneficial for their health. The timing is incredible to create wealth. Not only a health and wealth opportunity, but for us personally it is a business opportunity that we have shared and taught the principals with our growing team. They have done the same thing we have taught them with their contacts, this time with THEIR goals in mind. We have read, listened, traveled to hear and learn from Dr Titus, Randy Schroeder and other leaders in the industry. Our learning is a daily activity since we made the decision to engage in this business. It is personally rewarding to have built a team that has grown throughout many states with the international opportunity very near. We find value in knowing that our time invested in our team, answering questions, getting on a three-way call at any hour of the day, driving 6 hours and helping host a Brand Ambassador's first Kannaway event, which in turn helps build their business and our business. It is rewarding hearing that some we have introduced to the business have been able to purchase their braces, make a payment on a new vehicle that was badly needed or that there is peace in their home after a child no longer is experiencing bouts of anxiety since taking the product.

It is a concise, intentional decision to not live a mediocre life, but an active choice to help ourselves and help others help themselves. It doesn't matter what level of degree you graduated with, or even if you graduated. You must have the willingness and discipline to follow the steps. Simply follow the system that is being taught in this book. Along with following the steps, come personal and business development skills. Success in Kannaway does not occur by chance. There is no luck or guesswork involved. There is a proven and predictable pattern of activities (The 10 Steps to Success). You don't have to have those skills in order to start. We just borrowed the skills of our up line as we are developing the skills in ourselves. The skills are attainable for anyone who can read or watch a video. Read, learn and follow "The 10 steps" and commit to investing the time to DO the steps. This business is like a franchise without a gigantic franchise cost that most can't afford. There are no employees to manage. We just teach and point to the 10 steps for your team. It is a financial opportunity that we have shared with many and yet we have just started. This wheel for success has been invented already. Your age and your current income level do not matter. Whether or not you choose to take action does! I believe the ABSOLUTE best thing is the people this product is targeted for. Not just women or men or kids or grandparents. IT IS A CONSUMABLE PRODUCT FOR EVERYONE and their PETS! The 10 steps combined with a superior product that everyone needs with residual income that is built from helping others to build their team with a proven process is a WIN WIN!!!!!

Kyle and I were recently reflecting on our last 40 years of living and our financial well-being. We have lots of things on our bucket list to do, places to see and most importantly so many people and organizations we want to help, which all take MONEY!!! This Kannaway opportunity and the 10 Steps is a vehicle that anyone can drive successfully to obtain your financial goals---We are experiencing this for ourselves. Follow the 10 Steps!!!

"Sheer effort enables those with nothing- to surpass those with privilege and position."- Toyotomi Hideyoshi

Here's to the next 40 years! Be Blessed.

Bill and Roseann Decker - Iowa

We, along with my brother Brian opened the FIRST Kannaway CBD store in Iowa. The CBD is a life saver for me. I was on opioids since 1988. From 2007 to 2018 I was on them every single day. I was never able to quit taking them due to the pain from all the surgeries I had in 36 years while working at Tyson foods. We are so thankful we found the CBD and this company because I am now totally pain free as of December 2018. Most of my back pain, neck pain and shoulder pain were gone within 2 ½ months, but I had bursitis in my hips for 3 decades. Now I am totally pain free and I feel like I am 50 instead of 65! My wife's testimony is even more powerful than mine. I truly believe that everyone should be taking CBD. Now everyone's results are different, but the truth is- most feel so much better when consuming our products. They don't cure or treat disease but they do help the body to restore balance.

My name is Rosann and I want to share my story. My reason for needing CBD is that I have a long history of excruciating, disabling medical issues. My story actually started 20 years ago when I was diagnosed by a Rheumatologist with Fibromyalgia. Tricky to diagnose but doctor gave me Hydrocodone. I took that off and on for years and then decided I'd tough it out. That didn't last long. The pain was wrenching! I visited with my MD at least four times a year. Each visit, I was given a new med. Every single visit. I have tried the whole menu when it comes to meds. I have seen at least 15 doctors. I hit rock bottom about a year and a half ago. I often had UTI's even with all the meds, it didn't resolve and I turned septic. For me having sepsis, I lost memory, my ability to walk at times, my soul was depressed, and but once again the pain returned. At night, I would go online and talk to others in pain and feeling alone and misunderstood. To surround yourself with people whom also suffer is encouraging because there are days when to get out of bed is the goal for morning. To go to work and make it through the day is a miracle. I've prayed for this day although I really didn't believe I would see that day. I wanted to live- but not the life I was living.

My first words to my husband Bill was that I am a prime candidate to try Kannaway CBD and would be ruthlessly honest if it doesn't work. My first Kannaway product was Salve. Smelled soothing and I applied it to my joints. My gosh after about a week my hands and back felt relief. Next, I started using Kannaway Premium Oil. Wow, NO

MORE NERVE PAIN. (Restless legs is a horrific feeling especially when it moves to your upper body). Nothing has EVER touched that pain! So shocked when I can wake up and feel refreshed in a way I haven't felt in years. I give credit to this product and how it nourished my endocannabinoid system. Now, I also vape at night for sleeping. There is so much more to my story. I'm so GRATEFUL for the Kannaway family and leadership. Kannaway is 100% federally legal and I feel God has put it in my life! My hope is to connect with all of the people crying out for help. Kannaway will help so many people feel better!

Heidi Rapp Sarno - New Jersey

The foundation for my love of science and healthcare became apparent to me when I was in junior high school. My history teacher had given us the homework assignment of following a current topic in the newspaper that semester. We were to write a report on that topic and hand it in by the end of the semester. The topic I chose was 'Toxic Shock Syndrome'. It was all over the newspapers back then.

It's quite nice to look back and reflect on a teacher who truly made an impact on who I am today and what my interests are. For me that teacher was my high school biology teacher, Mr. D. Mr. D was such a wonderful role model. He was happy and positive, and truly an inspiring person. He made it very clear that he loved his job and he made sure that his students learned the course content. All of us kids loved and respected him. High school biology was an interesting subject for me however the best part, was that this high school biology teacher thoroughly enjoyed each and every one of his students. As a teenager we knew this, and because of his character and how he treated us, he became my all-time favorite teacher. Today 41 years later, I call him my friend.

Dentistry became my career choice. After 35 successful years of practicing in the field I decided to make some changes due to physical limitations and if I'm to be honest, I really needed a change. Burnout was obviously affecting me, so I accepted administration positions in a substance abuse facility and later in a hospital wound care center. There were also other positions in between. I was frantically trying to figure out where I fit in after all this time. One thing remained constant, my love for patients, and meeting new people. I have always enjoyed people of all ages and getting to know them.

A few years ago, my Mom was diagnosed with colon cancer. She thought she had back aches from working long hours at her job in furniture design. Mom passed away rather quickly. She was a very young Mom; she had me at 17 years old. Imagine being 21 years of age and having 4 children 5 years old and under? Wow, that is a handful! Before she passed away, she thanked me for helping her raise my three younger brothers. Taking care of people is ingrained in me and just what I do. So why am I telling you all this? The better question is, what am I not telling you?

Have you ever heard of the hamster wheel metaphor? The hamster wheel literally describes the concept of running in circles but making no progress. Doing things the same way, repeating the same mistakes, guided by a sense that motion is the important thing - I just needed to keep going. I had bills to pay. I could tell you more stories of what I had experienced and how I stayed too long in some of the positions I had worked in. I had way too many negative experiences working with coworkers, doctors and insurance companies that I'd rather not share. I felt exhausted, disappointed in people and was so completely burnt out, that I was ready to walk away from healthcare completely. On one particular very hard day I stopped at my local library to pick up a book I had reserved. I will never forget this day. The book was called Capital Gaines by Chip Gaines. Chip put into words the career and life experiences I had been experiencing yet I never knew how to communicate what was happening around me. In one particular chapter he wrote about 'Character Assassination' and 'Bridges'. This was just the right information I needed to read in that moment and the timing could not have been better. When Chip defined character assignation he literally gave me the gift of understanding what had been happening in quite a few of the offices that I had worked. Reading his words was like the light bulb being turned on in my head. Now I got it! "Capital Gaines" is a really great read that I highly suggest. He is an amazing business-man and he sure does know a lot about people and great relationships.

Now my Kannaway story:

On two or three occasions I remember a post coming across my Facebook page from a person by the name of Randy Schroeder. Randy is person I knew of from a previous network marketing company that I had been involved in. Randy's post was about Hemp CBD. When I read his FB post, I thought to myself, "What the heck is wrong with this guy? Doesn't he know that I am in the

healthcare field? I don't want anything to do drugs!"
Seriously, those were my thoughts. (I am so sorry Randy).
I had no idea that Hemp and Marijuana were two totally
different things. Wow, did I have a lot to learn! It was
about a year later that I read another post talking about
the very same topic. Hemp and CBD. But this time it was
Renita Rhone Brannan on FB. I was confused and
concerned but more willing to read what she had to say. I
remembered Renita from a previous network marketing
company as well. When I read Renita's posts, I paid
attention. She was such an inspiration for me. She was
positive and loving. Renita has energy just oozing from
every seam. She was a force to be reckoned with and I
just loved her. Unbeknownst to her, she saved me from
some very dark moments in my life. Renita literally had
no idea who I was other than a name on her Facebook
friends list, but when she posted and wrote on FB, I
listened. This one particular time Renita spoke of a health
scare that had to do with her son Beau. She mentioned
CBD. She talked about hemp. (That drug thing again) She
spoke of a continuing education course on CBD. That's
when I decided to learn more. I didn't like being in the
dark about this topic. I wanted to know more. Besides I
needed the continuing education credits to maintain my
dental hygiene licensure. So why not take the course?

I remember being in front of my laptop learning about
this system we have in our body called the
Endocannabinoid System. The what? How come I didn't
know this? I have had to take CE courses every year for
the last 35 years and I read my health journals all the time.
What was this ECS? Why had I never heard of this? I
reached out to two of my friends that had recently
graduated nursing school. "Did you learn about the ECS

in school?", I asked them. Both had no idea what I was talking about. I asked doctors that I worked with at the hospital. They didn't know much about it to comment. One doctor actually repeated after me, C. B. what? In the CE course I came across a section on how CBD may help our body with all sorts of health issues including fighting different kinds of cancer. I clearly heard myself say out loud, "Holy Sh*%!" Remember I had lost my Mom to colon cancer a few years before and colon cancer was one of the types of cancer the course was speaking of. Not only was I shocked, I was angry! I couldn't help but dive in and learn as much as I could about this most fascinating topic. Not only did I feel as if I was in college for a few months but I also did my due diligence and researched the premier CBD company called Kannaway. I began using their product when I learned that it may help with hormone balance. The hot flashes I had been experiencing were almost daily and I was starting to believe I just might self-combust into ashes one day (I'm not kidding). Since that first week of using Kannaway's Pure Gold CBD, I have not had one hot flash since. Not to mention better sleep, no more biting around my cuticles from anxiety, (who knew I had a form of anxiety!) and no more predicting the weather better than the weathermen. I had those predictions down to a science! I could tell when it was going to rain, when it was going to snow and what time of day. I kind of miss the predictions but I do not miss taking all the Tylenol and Advil. The best part, and this fills my eyes with tears a bit, was when my daughter came home from college in South Carolina and told me that I was a new person. "You are the Mom I used to know", she said. This is a true story.

So here I am a woman ready to walk away from

healthcare completely, not only because of the hamster wheel but for so many other crappy reasons. My list is long and a bit negative. I really don't want to go backwards, so I'll keep moving forward with this story. I remember Chip Gaines speaking of passion and when we feel passion to go after it. He said something about getting knocked down, but we have to keep going. Letting the punches keep us down is the biggest mistake we could make. And you know what? I believed him. I had a fire burning in my gut regarding all this new ECS and CBD information and I just wanted to tell everyone. I wanted to shout it from the rooftops. I came to the realization that I wouldn't be leaving the healthcare field any time soon.

I was fortunate to grow up with parents that weren't afraid to take risks and try new things. My Mom was a Martha Stewart times ten. My Dad was a machinist by trade and owned his own business. Dad is also an inventor. Mom and Dad together had vision and dreams. They were always ahead of the times and they tackled so many great projects together teaching me and my brothers along the way. This is probably the biggest and most important part of being the daughter of the parents I have, and had, that I just cherish. Dad is now 77 years old and when we recently spoke of Hemp and CBD, he shared with me that he would like to start growing hemp on his property up in New York State. I would love for him to meet Dr. Stuart Titus one day.

Fast forward to 2019, Just a few months, ago I celebrated the Grand Opening of Your Partner in Health at The CBD Wellness Center of New Jersey. I so missed having my Mom with me and all of her creativity. I do believe that she was with me in spirit though because these last 8-9 months I have never found so many pennies! Just to be clear, I wasn't looking for them. It had to be her, or God, or both I'd like to believe. Finding them at first was fun. I liked to read "In God We Trust" on each and every one of them. And it's a bonus when I'd find them on heads. But these last few months finding pennies had become so repetitive and odd to me. It was almost as if someone was saying 'pay attention'. I truly believe someone was looking out for me and making sure that I felt secure in knowing that I was on the right path and that I had some invisible guidance. Thank you, God. Thank you, Mom.

It's scary taking risks, but I am now using everything I have learned from my past and taking it to a new level. I feel exhilarated and so happy to be in this place. I am stepping up to the plate, taking responsibility to help educate people in this crazy new space of hemp CBD and I feel so honored to be part of such an important and rewarding movement in our history. Oh, and by the way, the biology teacher I told you about, Mr. D? He participated in my grand opening celebration and was standing right next to me while I helped the Mayor cut the ribbon in our ribbon cutting ceremony. Mr. D has one of the greatest testimonies about Kannaway CBD. Life is so good! ☺

Adam & Austin Berger – North Dakota

It was December 2019, my mother had just went through her 8th consecutive surgery on her stomach to try and replace the feeding tube that had been dislodged 7 times prior.

I never expected to see my mother on a feeding tube, especially at her age of just 55. However, the doctors had explained to us that because her stomach has been so lazy, it could be possible the stomach was paralyzed, and the food would not get digested If she was able to eat. Now, I'm not doctor, but instantly I thought, "So will she have to use this feeding tube the rest of her life?". In disbelief, I began to research, and research some more, until I stumbled across CBD and the wide range of benefits from CBD. The more I read, the more I was becoming a believer, but I also read about the many dangers of using just any CBD, so I had to find the right company. I was looking for a company I could trust, after all, I was giving this to my sick mother, who already has GI problems, so putting in something toxic could be fatal.

When you have so many consecutive surgeries and you are in the hospital as often as she was you became more susceptible to infection. She then got C. Diff. Colitis and was taken by ambulance back to Minneapolis. At this time, they did a barium swallow test and the test came back that the food still had not emptied in her stomach for 5 days. This led to the Surgeons belief that her stomach was paralyzed and she would solely depend on the feeding tube, which would now be surgically placed.

They decided they would allow her to go home to be treated so she wouldn't be at risk for another infection, but was told she must come back in 6 weeks or she will die of starvation and malnourishment.

This is when we were at our most desperate point, and eager to try anything that may help. CBD was the next option, we just had to find the right company.

The 3 things that made our family choose Kannaway: 1. The US Hemp Authority Seal 2.Triple-Lab-testing from seed to soil. 3. The Certificate of Analysis and Independent Lab Results for each product.

I chose the highest milligrams and highest concentration product they provide, Kannaway's Gold Oral Applicator.

After just 2 weeks her stomach felt more relaxed for the first time in years. She decided she could try and eat, starting with bone broth, shakes, smoothies and other soft foods.

Within one month the inflammation was improved, and the pain in her abdomen was significantly less.

Now 6 months later, she is back at work full-time and moving around better than she has for the last 6 years! If she doesn't have her CBD for 48 hours, it takes about 48 hours for her to feel relief again.

After we saw just how amazing this product worked for our mother, we decided to fully invest in Kannaway.

Because of CBD's amazing anti-inflammatory and anti-aging benefits, we knew it would be the perfect fit for our Medspa. Since we have brought on the CBD products, we have increased our daily ticket sales, as well as reached a new client base that was more willing to try all-natural products, a target market that may often be harder to reach for a Medical Spa. Due to the injection of revenue we were getting from the additional CBD sales, we decided we wanted to take it a little further, and develop our own protocol for the CBD Facial, one that would instantly provide results!

After a few weeks, and tons of research, we had developed our brand new, CBD Facial! We were so excited with the results we were getting that we decided we needed to share with our city, and what was the best way to directly invite them in and see what benefits this facial could do?!

Invite Renita in for a FACEBOOK LIVE! We instantly had people tuning in, asking questions, even calling to book before her treatment was over! By the end of the Live Video, we had generated hundreds of comments and likes! Within 6 days we had recorded an all-time high in facial bookings, 53!!! 53 CBD Facials book in less than one week! How many of your Spa/Med Spas could use 53 clients in one week?

For those of you wondering what company you can trust with your family, and your business, Kannaway is the natural choice! If you are interested in our CBD Facial protocol or any questions about selling CBD in your Medspa or Spa, please don't hesitate to reach out!

Connie Pickar – North Dakota

If asked two years ago if I would be network marketing, I probably would have said, "Heck no! That's a pyramid scheme!"

The unique and powerful health benefits of CBD and the timing unlike anything I'd witnessed before changed everything!

I've always tried to take care of myself, eat well, PFC, exercise and get proper sleep. When I heard about CBD and did my research, I knew it was something I wanted to add to my health routine.

I joined Kannaway in January 2018 and started using their products for overall and preventative health. Within the first week, I could already feel and see changes for the greater good.

I noticed I was sleeping like a baby, content and peaceful all night. Restful sleep hadn't happened in years. Most nights I would wake with restless legs or needing the restroom. I was on prescription anti-anxiety and depression medication for a few years due to life events. About two months after CBD, I could tell my mood was great, ZERO ANXIETY! Holy buckets, that was huge because I would worry about everything out of my control. Lord knows we can't control everything, but I always felt like I needed to!

After seeing these incredible personal changes, I had to share CBD with others. In November 2018 I went all in working my CBD business, quickly advancing up the ranks. Every day I'd hear from customers how much better they were feeling. This made me push harder to share and educate about CBD. Remember, I was one who had never been in network marketing before. By consuming Kannaway CBD, educating myself, following the company's 10 steps, and participating in weekly webinars, it became something I really enjoyed. I attended presentations, held my own presentations and went to conferences. I was helping so many people and I was really having fun!

My story isn't over.

April 26, 2019 my life changed forever. This Friday was just like any other. Going through my daily routine and spreading CBD love. At noon of this particular Friday, I was taking my husband lunch as I did every day. Only this day, I was greeted by other employees along with the county sheriff.

My Husband of 22 years had taken His life. He was my everything.

If you have experienced a traumatic loss, you can understand the heartache, tears, stress, and total loneliness that comes with it. How do I go on?

I put it all in God's hands. Friends and family were so supportive. Some suggested I get on sleep aids and anxiety medications. I told them I would rather stick with CBD and increase my serving from 50mg to 200mg per day. One thing that will never change is the love I will always have for my first true love. But Kannaway CBD has helped me sleep again, have some clarity and process emotions of it all much better.

Three weeks after my husband's passing my brother was diagnosed with lymph node cancer. To say I was angry with the world and God is an understatement. How could he do this to me? How am I supposed to deal with this too? I'll tell you how. You take a deep breath, get on your knees and ask our Lord for HELP. Everyday believing in

God's plan. Putting one foot in front of the other. You'll stumble and you'll fall but God's love and grace will pick you up again.

With my Brothers diagnosis, I knew he needed CBD immediately. He started taking 500mg of two oral applicators and I continued 200mg of pure gold oil. CBD has helped my brother with appetite, nausea and sleep. All things that are affected by the poison called Chemo. It's been a true blessing. My brother is fighting the devil and I am right by his side.

I have met so many families through this journey and I share my knowledge of CBD with them. Praying that they will give it a try to help them through the battle of cancer.

During this time my CBD business has continued. I'm so grateful that network marketing and Kannaway CBD has allowed me to be with my family at these difficult times.

What's the next chapter hold for me and my family? Stay tuned. The best is yet to come.

Mariah Prussia – North Dakota

What is optimal health, and how can an individual structure their life to achieve it? Before diving into the depth of reaching optimal health, I would like to introduce myself and what I have found in my 20+ years in the health and wellness industry.

My name is Mariah Prussia, and I am a strong female who wears a plethora of hats, which include being a professional MMA fighter and boxer, personal trainer, motivational speaker, self-defense instructor, radio show host, certified nutrition coach and more. Each of my accolades have provided a segue into fulfilling my mission of empowering individuals, one rep at a time, one voice at a time!

As a fitness professional, professional athlete and business owner, it is not only essential but a necessity to be running on full cylinders; which includes enhancing one's knowledge on how to adequately fuel the mind and body. In recent months, I was introduced to an unfamiliar system found within our body, which is the largest regulatory system called the endocannaboid system. I know what you're thinking, what in the h#ll is that system and "why" haven't I heard of it before. You are not alone!!! I was very intrigued to learn more, so I booked a flight to California to listen Dr. Stuart Titus, PhD. Dr. Stuart Titus broke down the properties, the direct connection the endocannaboid system has with gastrointestinal system and central nervous system, along with how individuals can increase the efficiency of the regulatory system through pure CBD oil. After doing research on the Kannaway products, patents and utilizing echoconnection.org to review additional articles on pertinent health concerns, I knew that incorporating Kannaway Pure CBD Oil was a necessity for my internal health. What I found since implementing CBD into my regimen is, improved sleep, increased productivity and focus throughout the day, and finally, decreased inflammation. I have always had issues hitting REM sleep, and after taking CBD oil nightly, I sleep throughout the night and wake up feeling rested. In addition to the physical and mental benefits of Kannaway, I looked further into the financial potential after becoming a believer and a product of the product. After reviewing the compensation plan, I recognized the unlimited financial potential that would compliment my health and wellness clients, business and family. When you can provide health and wealth to the individuals in your life, it is then that you find the freedom to LIVE the life you have envisioned. To learn more about Kannaway, women's self-defense, motivational speaking and additional services I provide go to mariahprussia.com or FB mariahmpxprussia. To LIVE is to GIVE!

Jill Balzer – North Dakota

I can honestly say CBD has changed my life. My health and wellness journey started in January 2016 when my family and I were on a cruise ship. I ended up getting so sick, I was actually wheelchaired off the ship. It turned out that my liver was shutting down which is crazy to me because I always associated liver disease with alcohol, and I am not a drinker. I ended up doctoring for many weeks and was diagnosed with a viral infection. I feel like that is a term used when they don't know what is wrong with you. Shortly after, I was diagnosed with Hashimotos, a thyroid autoimmune disease. On top of that, I have struggled with severe anxiety most of my life. Between the thyroid and liver illnesses, I had zero energy. My life consisted of going to work and only doing the absolute necessities at home. I didn't want to do any extracurricular activities and I honestly didn't want to leave the house. I was basically bone-tired all the time. Even fun family outings would fill me with dread as I knew how miserable I would be after doing too much.

In 2017, at the advice of my chiropractor I gave up

gluten, dairy, grains and soy. I had also been sugar free for 4.5 years. I feel like it helped heal my gut, but it wasn't the "cure all" I was hoping for. Eating better improved my thyroid levels a bit but it didn't make me feel a whole lot better.

Then one day in January 2018 my sister-in-law introduced me to CBD. I attended a neighbor's home party and I was in awe listening to the presenter speak about CBD. I wondered if it was my missing link! I ordered and the rest is history. Within 2 weeks, I knew I needed this supplement, this gift from God. I started with experiencing more energy, then more focus. My sleep improved greatly and I was no longer waking up every night at 3 am to use the bathroom when my "worrier" would turn on and I couldn't turn it off so I would barely sleep the rest of the night. I stopped nagging my family which was HUGE. My anxiety went from over the top crazy worrying all the time to an occasional moment of having an anxious thought. My husband said I was a different woman!!! It has helped my marriage and helped my whole family. I seriously cannot say enough about what it has done for me and my family's health.

One of my favorite benefits of taking CBD is I've even started up my creative side business, "The Farmer's Daughters" again. I am painting, creating and even overcome my fear of being in front of a camera. I am doing Facebook lives teaching some tips and tricks in the creative world. I thought my creative days were over but turns out I am just getting started. Projects that scared me before I became sick are now being tackled with excitement and gusto. My most recent project is painting my cabinets which is no small task.

The financial opportunity is incredible with Kannaway. I initially started to get healthy, but I ended up sharing my story with others. I am earning commission from Kannaway when people join our amazing team and order products as brand ambassadors or customers. I quickly grew my business enough to earn enough to pay for our products and now we are paying off our extra debt with Kannaway's monthly "Minimum Income Guarantee"! Talk about a life changing benefit! I never considered a network marketing business before and now I get to share my story and help others get well. It is so rewarding! I am so grateful to have this opportunity and invite you to join us!

Kriss and Doug Pavik – Minnesota / Florida

After a bad breakup with a former Network Marketing company I swore I would never join another. Then my dog got sick, and when a family member gets sick you do what you can to help them. I was directed to CBD by a girlfriend of mine who just completed treatment for breast cancer. It was recommended to her, but she never sought it out. I researched quickly as I knew I didn't have much time. I found Kannaway. Their products were triple lab tested, they had been around a long time and they had research, substantial scientific research.

As soon as the product arrived, I started my dog on CBD. After all the research, I knew it would be beneficial for me as well. After the first couple of weeks, the difference was already amazing for both my dog and me! It was so incredible that I announced on Facebook, "I am ALL IN" and ready to launch something new!

When I started this business, this was my life; I was working a full-time job, one I hated, the stress was horrible, and I needed out. I was living in a town that, well frankly, I hated. We lived in the middle of nowhere, nothing to do and the weather was dreadful in the winter, bitterly cold sometimes -40 below. My husband and I were also working on rehabbing a home as we purchased a fixer upper. When we weren't working our day jobs, we were working on the house so it was livable. I was busy, we were busy, and now I'm going to add a business into the mix? YES!

I purchased the Kannaway Total Product Experience package so I could experience all the products and represent them well to others. I quickly enrolled my first 3 people and became fast start qualified, before I knew what fast start qualified was. I then learned the business by watching the videos, learning the ten steps to success and building my WHY so large it could not be ignored. Our team grew and the goal was to get everyone on our team fast start qualified, holding their hand for thirty days and then letting them fly. Before I knew it, I had hit my first Kannaway Minimum Income Guarantee (MIG) of $500 per month!

I continued working the business and as our team grew, we just linked arms, again getting them started right in the first 30 days and helping them determine their "why". Soon after hitting my first MIG, I made it to the next rank, AREA Director. The minimum income guarantee was $2500 per month, I almost couldn't believe it. My team was growing, they were moving and hitting their MIG. The journey with Kannaway is amazing. Anyone can do this if they have a WHY.

My WHY, was big, I wanted to move some place warm, more people, more things to do. Most of all I wanted time with my husband, that wasn't work. I wanted to vacation with him. I also knew how stressed he was at work and I wanted to make enough money that if he needed to quit his job he could.

My husband quit his job 4 months ago and we are in no rush for him to find a new one. He may even go back to school. Last month we picked out our retirement home. This month they are finishing construction. Next month we move into our forever home, moving from Northern Minnesota to Cape Coral, Florida only a few miles from the Gulf. I feel very blessed to be part of Kannaway and to continue this journey with friends.

Find me on FACEBOOK (Kriss K Pavik) or TWITTER @krisskk as I'd love to connect and help you join our fast-growing team!

Liz Diehl - Oregon

I am Liz Diehl, my life has changed because Kannaway stepped into my life in 2018. I have been all about natural health for years. Well, let me say that I have heard the 3 scariest little words "You Have Cancer" in my lifetime. And, I have not only heard them once, but twice! Once you hear those words they can't be taken back, you must move forward. Thank goodness I had started a journey of health a few years prior. So, my personal health research had already started. Pair that research with my love for the network marketing industry and a marriage is born.

Having raised my sons in Eugene, OR and living now in Seattle with my husband, my awareness around the Cannabis Industry was peaked. I started searching for a way to be involved with this gorgeous nutrient, CBD from Hemp. How could I create an income stream and drench myself in CBD?

The company Kannaway kept rising to the top as the leader in the industry. With this info I took the plunge. When looking for any venture it is always smart to be at the right place, at the right time, with the right team. Never again will we experience the end of the prohibition of cannabis. This is the right place, the right time, and Kannaway is the right team.

It is a beautiful thing to create income while getting healthy and blessing others. CBD has had a major impact on my life, my health, and those I love. Never again do I want to hear those 3 little scary words. So, cheers to Kannaway and cheers to those who walk this earth with an open mind. It will take you far!

ECHOCONNECTION Director- Andrea Barnes

Please research all of the studies on
www.echoconnection.org Our CBD has blessed so
many people due to this organization.

"One person can make a difference, and every person
must try." -John F. Kennedy

From ECHO Connection:

Emergency hospital visits, missed work, and emotional
turmoil—families coping with critical illness need
tremendous support to deal with these everyday
challenges. Traditional healing pathways often fall short
and leave these families seeking alternative methods to
improve their health and well-being.

Freda is a young mother living in Mississippi raising five
beautiful children. Shortly after her youngest son Jonah
was born, she realized something wasn't right. Blonde-
haired, blue-eyed Jonah wasn't developing at the same
rate as his older siblings. He couldn't sleep. He hurt
himself and others and faced significant learning delays.
By the time Freda reached out to ECHO, her family was
in crisis.

David is a Gulf War veteran still suffering from the
strains of war. Since his return, he has received on-going
medical care, and lives with frustrating medical setbacks
and ineffective prescriptions. A recent medication he tried
caused him to shake. Because of prescription side-effects
and several chronic conditions, he had to step down from
serving as a constable in his hometown. His family has

suffered with him and David's constant medical needs took a tremendous financial toll on the family. They reached out to ECHO because traditional medical pathways were not giving David the life he deserved.

Jenny has suffered from health issues nearly her entire adult life. Her chronic conditions haunt and invade her day-to-day living. Recently, she got the diagnosis everyone fears, but even though her own health is fragile, Jenny must also care for her elderly mother. No matter how ill Jenny feels, her mother still needs her daily assistance—picking up groceries, making meals, and accompanying her to appointments. By the time she reached out to ECHO, Jenny was desperate.

These stories reflect the health and living realities of ECHO families. Our clients come from all walks of life and live broadly across the United States, Europe, Mexico and Brazil. We serve children through older adults.

Our mission is to serve families facing severe illnesses who are seeking the therapeutic properties of CBD Oil. Financially, the oil is beyond their means, and their need is great.

ECHO stands for Education, Collaboration and Hope.

- Education: ECHO aims to educate the world about the benefits and science of cannabinoids. A tremendous amount of research is being conducted throughout the world, revealing more about CBD, other cannabinoids, and cannabinoid science. ECHO is building the world's largest library of this research for easy, free access to anyone looking for more information.

- Collaboration: ECHO hosts an online community where people can collaborate and learn about CBD from each other in a safe and non-judgmental environment.
- Hope: ECHO provides hope for those dealing with difficult health issues. Hope is the giving branch for ECHO, and this is where you can make a difference financially.

When donors support ECHO Connection, they help us to add to and expand our medical and education page. They aid our ability to build a meaningful community that supports individuals seeking support and information. Finally, they help to provide the means for natural healing to families who need it most.

Visit us at **www.echoconnection.org**

Final look at Kannaway and MJNA and their portfolio of incredible companies!

When you launch your Kannaway CBD business and when you consume Kannaway CBD you are part of something incredibly special and unique. You are part of a powerful mission and movement that is changing the healthcare system in the US and changing the household income status for families across this great nation!

When we say Kannaway is a company of firsts:

First and only CBD company in PDR (Physician's Desk/Digital Reference)

First and Only CBD to receive licensing rights to patent #6630507 -NIH patent on Cannabidiol (Kannalife Sciences)

First Publicly Traded Cannabis Company in U.S. – MJNA

First company to create 100% THC products adhering to WADA (world anti-doping association) standards

First company to triple lab test and third-party lab test

First and only company asked to speak to WHO (World Health Organization) on CBD in 2017

Dr Stuart Titus, our founder, educated FDA at hearing on CBD on May 31st

Largest non-profit online resource document research library to look cannabis studies, CBD- Thousands of scientific studies available. Echo has given $1,300,000 of our CBD to families in need

First company to have non psychoactive hemp CBD products available in United States, Entire EU, Japan, Russia and Vietnam

Hemp meds (our sister company) is already being prescribed in Paraguay, Brazil, Mexico as a pharmaceutical for the treatment of several conditions

One of the first companies to receive US Hemp authority seal from the US Hemp Round Table

Kannaway was invited to join United States Hemp Roundtable

QR code on every one of our products to take you to the exact COA (certificate of analysis)

10 ways of earning income PLUS stock incentive from MJNA

Affordable, legal startup

Immediate website and Kannaway Connect app to work your business from your phone

Kannaway named TOP CBD MLM Company in 2020 by HealthMJ

Utilizes organic, sustainable, and environmentally responsible farming practices

Unique cultivars located in Holland which are high-CBD, non-GMO hemp

Incredible trip incentives

Monthly free product available for Brand Ambassadors

Incredible free business training

Taking part in explosive cannabis industry-$600 million in 2018, 22 billion by 2022 and 57 billion by 2025

Tax efficiency

Work from home, phone, computer

Hundreds of NFL, NBA, NFL, professional athletes on Kannaway products

Featured on NBC, Fox News, Dateline, The Doctors, ABC, CBD, Forbes, History Channel, and dozens more

Partnered with **www.endocannahealth.com** - DNA testing to determine which cannabinoid you are deficient in.

CALL TO ACTION:

Reach out to me or the person who handed you this book to launch your business. Get ready for an awesome adventure! Your willingness to put the steps in the book to work will determine your success. Make decisions today for growth and abundance. Seek out positive people who are open to opportunity and looking to win. Partner with those who are ready to be well and wealthy!

By thought, the thing you want is brought to you; by action you receive it.

The very BEST is yet to come!! 2020 is YOUR year to create your CBD Money Tree!!

God bless you and may you receive the courage and strength to serve and bless others!

Scott, Renita, Beau, Truitt, Rocco, and Zoe Brannan

ABOUT THE AUTHOR

Renita Brannan is passionate about the nourishment of her family. Renita and her husband Scott have three boys, Beau, Truitt, and Rocco and a sweet girl dog name Zoe- all who consume Kannaway CBD!

Renita is a dedicated health and wealth leader. She is a disruptor in people living according to "status quo". She encourages people to "wake up" and "get up"! She believes in dreaming big and praying even bigger. With persistent and consistent effort coupled with the right attitude, all things are possible.

She has been a health leader for over 23 years. Her first breaking out of "status quo" was being the only female in the weight room when she was 14 years old. That passion has continued throughout her life. Renita is certified to teach over 20 different modalities of fitness/health and has traveled the world as a Master Trainer certifying instructors to teach various forms of exercise. In addition, she is a Certified Nutrition Coach, in which she helped the state of ND to lose 100,000 lbs of fat. She has been featured on CNN HLN for Testimony Tuesday due to the immense health successes of all ages she was working with. In addition, Renita is the health and fitness expert for the North Dakota's NBC affiliate, KFYR-TV for the past 7 years. Every week she addresses health, nutrition, and fitness topics to educate the viewers to take charge of their health with Wellness Wednesday. Renita also co-authored an Amazon best seller, Nice and Fat to help people break out of the dieting madness.

Renita is a sought-after public speaker in the areas of health and business. She has delivered thousands of presentations helping people to live life fully.

Renita recently created the PFC Plate, the world's first nutritional blood sugar stabilization tool to help individuals rewire their brains through repetition to nourish their bodies with food. In a recent clinical study, 19.8 inches of body fat were lost in 8 weeks. This was in addition to a significant reduction in A1C. In addition, she just launched a PFC bar to aid in the process of health, vitality, and weight loss. www.pfcplate.com

Renita has pioneered the CBD industry in North Dakota and across the US. She played an integral role in educating state legislators. This led to rewriting ND state century codes, differentiating hemp CBD from marijuana. She has launched a CBD revolution throughout the US and now the world and invites you to join on this powerful once in a lifetime mission!

Made in the USA
Monee, IL
17 February 2020